Ghosts, Ghouls, & Monsters of Long Island

The Paranormal Adventurers
Joseph Flammer & Diane Hill

Schiffer ®
Publishing Ltd
4880 Lower Valley Road • Atglen, PA 19310

Published by Schiffer Publishing, Ltd.
4880 Lower Valley Road
Atglen, PA 19310
Phone: (610) 593-1777; Fax: (610) 593-2002
E-mail: Info@schifferbooks.com

For the largest selection of fine reference books on this and related subjects,
please visit our website at: **www.schifferbooks.com**
You may also write for a free catalog.

This book may be purchased from the publisher.
Please try your bookstore first.

We are always looking for people to write books on new and related subjects.
If you have an idea for a book, please contact us at
proposals@schifferbooks.com

Schiffer Books are available at special discounts for bulk purchases for sales promotions or premiums. Special editions, including personalized covers, corporate imprints, and excerpts can be created in large quantities for special needs. For more information contact the publisher.

In Europe, Schiffer books are distributed by
Bushwood Books
6 Marksbury Ave.
Kew Gardens
Surrey TW9 4JF England
Phone: 44 (0) 20 8392 8585; Fax: 44 (0) 20 8392 9876
E-mail: info@bushwoodbooks.co.uk
Website: www.bushwoodbooks.co.uk

Other Schiffer Books by the Author:
Long Island's Most Haunted: A Ghost Hunter's Guide,
978-0-7643-3293-7, $14.99
Long Island's Most Haunted Cemeteries, 978-0-7643-3589-1, $24.99

Other Schiffer Books on Related Subjects:
Spooky Creepy Long Island, 978-0-7643-2814-5, $12.95

Library of Congress Control Number: 2012942957

Designed by Mark David Bowyer
Type set in Humanist521 BT / New Baskerville BT

ISBN: 978-0-7643-4126-7
Printed in the United States of America

Contents

Acknowledgments

As with all our books, we owe a great deal of gratitude to artist Karen Isaksen of Bay Shore for her contributions of drawings. Thank you, Karen.

We are also grateful to the library directors and librarians across Long Island and in New York City for their continued support. Thank you for inviting us to speak in your auditoriums and giving us the opportunity to share with the public information about ghosts, strange beings, and paranormal phenomena that is taking place right now on Long Island.

Likewise, we thank many fellow investigators who have contributed their knowledge, photos, and experiences, or whose work we refer to in this book. This includes references to extraordinary voice transmissions received on Mount Misery Road by members of the Long Island Paranormal Investigators (LIPI). The bone-chilling transmissions were presented in a feature on WPIX Channel 11 News in 2010. LIPI members were kind enough respond to our request for a copy of the video of the news program. We refer to these amazing transmissions in a chapter about Mount Misery Road. Thank you, LIPI, and congratulations on all of your truly outstanding successes!

Thanks also goes out to psychic John Altieri, of North Babylon, who never fails to blow us away with his extraordinary psychic insights, experiences, and photographs of paranormal phenomena. We have much work to do to with you and members of The Babylon Paranormal Group in the future, John.

Also thanks goes out to psychic Ruth Bahr of Franklin Square, a member of Long Island Ghost Seekers. Your psychic visions led us to the alleged all-black Guardian creature of the Old Quaker Burying Ground in Farmingdale during the electrifying Long Island Devil Investigation, and for that we take off our hats and say thank you! Your communication with the supposed ghost of murder victim Nellie Backerd was shocking and profound. We look forward to working with you again to uncover more of the amazing story you relayed to us from Nellie's spirit.

Psychic Joe Cahill of Lindenhurst was invaluable during the Long Island Devil Investigation and the Potter's Field Investigation in the fall of 2010 and we could not thank you more. Investigators are now trying to learn more about the mass graves you and other psychics have possibly detected in the nearby woods while psychically sensing the ghosts of old Potter's Field graveyard.

We would especially like to thank members of the Long Island Paranormal Seekers (LIPS), whom we have joined on nighttime investigations of Sweet Hollow Road, Mount Misery, the Old Quaker Burying Ground, and Potter's Field Cemetery; members Kevin Kelly, William (Bill) Berongi, and Keith Baecker know the terrain of Sweet Hollow Road and Mount Misery and the ghosts that dwell within as well as any humans could. You uncovered paranormal phenomena during the Long Island Devil Investigation and made contact with the spirits at Potter's Field. We appreciate your guidance and friendship, and look forward to future midnight investigations with you.

Caesar Santos of West Islip is a dedicated paranormal investigator who commands our respect for going out in the night and photographing graveyards, and other haunted places, often with amazing results that draw the attention of even the most experienced spirit photographers. Caesar is always willing to share his understanding of the supernatural and explain how he gets spirits to materialize for his camera. In that way, Caesar, you are a true teacher. I know we have learned much from you, including the meaning of ghostly echolalia, i.e. spirits mimicking human voices. Your photos are spine-tingling and an inspiration for us.

Our thanks to T. Peter Park of Garden City South: You were an amazing help during the Long Island Devil Investigation. Your contributions of similar cases all over the world placed the Long Island Devil in a context that helped us all see we are dealing with an alleged creature that has been seen before in other places. Thank you for all your help, Peter.

To sisters-in-law Denise Reilly of West Babylon and Denise Reilly of Little Neck, and also Elizabeth Johnson of Floral Park, with whom we have investigated several locations, including the Long Island Devil Investigation, Potter's Field, and Sweet Hollow Road: We want you to know how much we respect your fortitude and perseverance as investigators, braving the night and sometimes difficult physical circumstances in an effort to document paranormal phenomena. We have all formed an invaluable team that we hope will to continue into the future. To Denise Reilly of West Babylon, we must comment on your perfect attendance during the Long Island Devil Investigation. Your seriousness and intelligent reflection of what you witnessed at the old graveyards makes you an investigator we trust, but being there one hundred percent of the time and leading others is what makes you a pillar of strength we personally depend on.

The same thanks goes out to Patrick Kenney of Farmingdale, Richard Widmann of Bay Shore, and Kenneth Widman of Bay Shore. We are so thankful for your friendship and thoughtful perseverance at getting to the truth of the "other side." We hope to continue our investigations of Long Island with you. We must add a special note of thanks to Patrick Kenney for your bravery in standing up and speaking the truth about the creature you witnessed in a tree in Farmingdale that launched the Long Island Devil Investigation. Your courage inspires us. Thank you, Patrick. You're a local hero!

To Mark and David Koenigsmann, a father and son ghost hunting team with whom we have investigated numerous locations, we must convey our most sincere respect for your tireless devotion to detecting spiritual activity in graveyards and other haunted locations. If paranormal investigators ever crack the secrets of the other side, it will be through intrepid ghost hunters such as yourselves that we do it. You guys rock!

Dee-Dee Phillips of Dix Hills and Ashley Pappas of Farmingdale are diligent investigators, keeping an eye out for creatures in the woods of Bethpage State Park from their view-point at the Bethpage Stables, located inside the park. We thank you for your work in capturing images of a strange black being with red eyes in the woods in the night and your contributions of information.

To Peggy Vetrano of Southampton and William Sanchez of Eastern Suffolk Paranormal — true leaders in the research of Long Island paranormal phenomena: We look forward to seeing in what new ways you will challenge our thinking and lead us to new levels of investigating ghosts. We continue to look to you for guidance and direction. We know we can trust your judgments to be well grounded, intelligent, and sound. Thank you for teaching us new techniques to reach the spirits. Also, to all members of Eastern Suffolk Paranormal, we want you to know what a pleasure it is to work with knowledgeable, intelligent, and personable investigators such as yourselves. We look forward to investigating with you again and again.

To Brigid Goode of Gettysburg, Pennsylvania, and Chris Griffith of Lake Ronkonkoma, both of the group the Paranormal Investigators; John and Michele Snow of Snow Family Paranormal of Baldwin; George Mendoza of Kings Park; and Donna Hahnan of Central Islip, we say thank you for being good friends. Those of you with whom we investigated haunted locations, such as Sweet Hollow Road, Potter's Field Cemetery, Pine Hollow Cemetery, and haunted houses, know what a great team we are when we're all together doing what we all love to do best. You guys are the best!

Most especially, we thank the forty hardy investigators of the Long Island Devil Investigation — the largest paranormal investigation ever to be conducted on Long Island — who contributed to this book with insights and their haunting experiences. Many of these investigators are mentioned above.

The Long Island Devil Investigation took place over the course of six investigative sessions during a three-month period in the spring of 2010. As investigators, we endured bugs, heat, humidity, and a rigorous schedule of meetings to search the night for the Long Island Devil, an all-black creature in a cape and hood that allegedly haunts the cemeteries of the Old Quaker Burying Ground in Farmingdale. Not only did we conclude the investigation with a lot of new and extraordinary paranormal experiences under our belts, but we also made many new and great friends who shared in a truly once in a lifetime adventure of which we should all be proud. Amazing things happened in the graveyards on those steamy nights and such a fantastic — and even historic — investigation can never be replicated. You were all part of it and made it happen. Congratulations!

While other people might have been regulars at the Long Island Devil Investigation sessions, we are listing only those investigators who completed a waiver for our publisher. The core Long Island Devil Investigation experts are as follows:

John Altieri, North Babylon; Keith Baecker, Roslyn Heights; Ruth Bahr, Franklin Square; William Berongi, Massapequa Park; Joe Cahill, Lindenhurst; John Cipriano, Levittown; Leslie Dann, Forest Hills; Scott Finz, Flushing; Michael Houze, Huntington Station; Elizabeth Johnson, Floral Park; Kevin Kelly, Massapequa Park; David Koenigsmann, Massapequa Park; Mark Koenigsmann, Massapequa Park; Patrick Kenney, Farmingdale; T. Peter Park, Garden City South; Alana Mancini, East Meadow; Dee-Dee-Philips, Dix Hills; Christine Re, Levittown; Denise Reilly, Little Neck; Denise Reilly, West Babylon; William Sanchez, Elmont; Lauren Sharkey, Lindenhurst; David VanderWerf, Elmont; Peggy Vetrano, Southampton; Kenneth Widman, Bay Shore; Richard Widmann, Bay Shore

We also wish to thank the following people for contributing stories, information, and research:

Lisa Barrow, Speonk; Diana Beller, Shirley; R. L. Demri, Central Islip; John Dickson, Levittown; Gabe Falsetta, Levittown; Mary Hull, King's Park; Jim Kenny, North Bellmore; Amanda Prag, Lindenhurst; Janet Russell, Medford; and Carmela Somma, Manorville

Do you see the face of the entity looming behind Diane Hill? This ghostly form and several others hovered over and around Diane while she was photographing the empty canyon of road between the trees on Sweet Hollow Road in Melville at night. Notice the line of white material extending from the apparition's snout to the ground. This might be the very material once widely known as "ectoplasm," the milky material mediums once claimed spirits used to materialize. Also notice the dark line cutting through the material to the right of the ghost's face. This line extends from the ground upwards to another apparition above Diane that was outside the view of the camera, but seen by Joseph Flammer at that moment.

Introduction

By Joseph Flammer

You probably believe in ghosts. Polls reveal most people do; however, you might not believe in ghouls and monsters.

The people of Baltimore didn't believe in them either and that's why in 1951 vigilante citizens with guns and clubs banded together with Baltimore police to patrol the dark alleyways and nighttime rooftops in the city to try to catch an insane "man."

Meanwhile, this supposed man, who was actually an inexplicable creature in all-black resembling the Grim Reaper in a cape and hood, caused people to fear for their safety when they traveled the streets at night. This was especially true for women walking alone. You never knew when the crazy man of Baltimore might jump out at you! Many people hid indoors at night.

This went on for three straight weeks.

It seemed the entity causing all the trouble stalked the wet streets of the city suddenly and from out of nowhere. The Baltimore phantom was seen flying from rooftop to rooftop like a blood-thirsty Dracula. It chased crying women and screaming girls.

When the creature's angry pursuers got too close, the entity simply vanished into the curling white mists of forgotten cemeteries. Therein old brown gravestones lay slantwise and broken in the tall wet grasses and spidery bushes. Nightly, the phantom disappeared amongst the wormy graves and neglected tombs in these burying grounds. No one could ever catch it... because it *wasn't* human!

Once folks realized they were not dealing with a human lunatic but something *other*, it quickly became apparent that whatever they were pursuing possessed near-mystical abilities. Who would have suspected at the outset that they were dealing with a supernatural entity that could jump to incredible heights and fly though the air for distances no human could possibly span with even the most powerful of leaps.

Perhaps it was a prehistoric creature that emerged from the depths of the dark Atlantic after sleeping for millennia, for Baltimore is on the eastern seaboard of the United States and the tides do bring into the city whatever the ocean wills, good or bad.

Perhaps the creature came from the thick woods of Maryland, wherein, legends say, the Blair Witch and other hellish creatures have been snatching children and adults for centuries, presumably to devour, bones and all.

Wherever it came from, the terrifying Baltimore creature would eventually be called the Phantom of O'Donnell Heights. Not unexpectedly, the elusive abomination was never caught. The last time it was chased, it slipped into a dark cemetery, opened the heavy stone lid to a musty sarcophagus, a dusty tomb, and disappeared inside, closing the lid over itself.

From there it's supposed the phantom went back from whence it came. Back to the dark dwelling place of the primordial black void to which all things must go... Back to Death.

When inspected, the stone encasement held cargo of dusty bones, matted hair, the smell of old, rotted flesh, and encrusted blood. There was no sign that the ghoul had ever stepped inside.

Clearly, the Phantom of O'Donnell Heights qualifies as a ghoul, but what is the definition of a ghoul? The *Merriam-Webster Dictionary* defines it as "an evil being that robs graves and feeds off the flesh of the dead."

While Long Island certainly does have a history of the type of ghouls that rob graves, eating the dead might be another story. For example, Suffolk County Police are still at a loss as to why a team of organized grave robbers broke into a mausoleum at St. Charles Cemetery in Farmingdale in August 2010 and stole the remains of an 87-year-old woman whom they never knew. The incident led to a large-scale police investigation and much newspaper and television coverage. The police determined the body snatchers had pre-planned every detail of their outrageous and dishonorable crime. It seemed the grave robbers picked the old lady's remains because they couldn't get into other crypts that they tried first. This was not a random joke performed by drunken fraternity boys, the police said at the time.

In the 1980s, a Northport youth was reportedly caught red-handed in a small woodsy cemetery stealing the skull and hand of a buried corpse for use in Satanic rituals. In another case, on June 16, 1984, Ricky Kasso, a youth who had just turned eighteen, went on to kill an acquaintance, seventeen-year-old Gary Lauwers, in the Aztakea Woods of Northport by stabbing him over thirty times in the face and chest, burning him in a small fire, and possibly even shoving rocks down his throat.

Kasso supposedly killed Lauwers in retaliation for stealing ten bags of PCP out of his jacket as he slept at a party.

As he conducted the murder, carving into Lauwer's eyeballs with his knife, Kasso demanded, "Say you love Satan!"

Kasso was reportedly stoned on mescaline, but some people at the time said it was probably LSD he had eaten that night, not mescaline. Also tripping were two other teenagers who accompanied Kasso and Lauwers into the woods and witnessed the killing. This murder took place in the same junky woods where Kasso believed he once saw Satan. Reportedly, one of the witnesses to the killing said he saw the trees of the woods bow submissively down to Kasso as he gouged into Lauwer's cheeks.

"Say you love Satan!" Kasso screamed again at the dying boy.

Lauwers responded, "I love my mother!"

Kasso stabbed Lauwers again, hitting the bone of his eye socket.

"Say you love Satan!"

"I love my mother!"

For two weeks following the gruesome killing, Kasso brought as many as thirty acquaintances to visit Lauwer's corpse as it decayed in the late June and early July heat in the open air of the woods. The kids who saw the gelatin-like body were sworn to secrecy to the Knights of the Black Circle, Kasso's self-styled stoner satanic cult, the press reported at the time. Two days after he was arrested for the murder, Kasso committed suicide in the Suffolk County Jail by hanging himself with a bed sheet tied to the upper bars of his cell door.

For the purposes of this book, we are defining "ghoul" not as a grave robber like Kasso or one who eats the flesh of the recent dead, but as the corpse of a dead human who escapes the grave to return to the world of the living.

How could this happen? Nobody knows, but ghouls have been mentioned in literature and folklore throughout history.

It's interesting to note that there has not been much research conducted on ghouls. Most sources, such as encyclopedias and dictionaries, merely point out that the term ghoul comes from the Arabic word "ghul."

"Ghoul – In popular legend a demonic being believed to inhabit burial grounds and other deserted places. In ancient Arabic folklore, ghuls belonged to a diabolical class of jinn (spirit) and were said to be the offspring of Iblis, the Muslim prince of darkness. They were capable of changing form, but their presence was always recognizable by their unalterable sign, ass's hooves...Anglicized as 'ghoul,' the word entered

English tradition and was further identified as a grave-robbing creature that feeds on dead bodies and on small children. In the West, ghouls have no specific image and have been described (by Edgar Allen Poe) as neither man nor woman...neither brute nor human."

-- *Encyclopedia Britannica*

Roget's College Thesaurus, on the other hand, provides the following synonyms for ghoul: grave-robber, body snatcher, demon, vampire, blackmailer, and evildoer. One must wonder what experiences people had with ghouls that led them to view ghouls as vampires. Obviously, ghouls have many flaws — and they're all associated with evil, killing, blood-sucking, and graves.

Maybe ghouls return to the world of the living to get our attention for some reason we cannot understand. It's more likely, though, that ghouls have not been conjured from the grave through their own efforts or intentions, but through the powers of unknown dark forces greater than mere human spirits, such as the legendary jinn. The term genie, a demon, comes from the term jinn. In folklore, a genie granted wishes to people so that it could lead them astray from their spiritual life, bringing them further away from redemption and God.

The dark forces that conjure corpses rule them, animating them for evil purposes; or it could be that a trickster entity animates a dead body to toy with mankind, possibly to lead humans away from God. Indeed, some societies believe trickster spirits can manipulate deceased humans out of the grave to curse and trick humans. The succubus and incubus are entities which, to this day, are believed by some people to have sex with the living, to corrupt their souls. Diane and I have investigated cases where people reported to us spirits had sex with them during the night, sometimes in front of other people. It's not uncommon to hear such victims say they enjoyed great sexual pleasure with these beings, though they despised the experiences.

During Medieval times, incubus and succubus entities were believed to be ghouls from the grave, possibly even composed from different parts of multiple dead bodies. The purpose of the succubus and incubus were to cause pure persons to fall into lust, for the evildoers were irresistible, bringing women and men to great climaxes, often performing perverse and unspeakable acts. It is believed, in some cases, these ghouls have had repeated sex with their victims — to the point that the humans died from exhaustion. Thus, ghouls probably do not carry anything of the personalities of the people who once occupied their corpses.

In fact, ghouls typically do not display any kind of love or sensitivity towards humans. Humanity and personality seem to have been sucked out of the corpses by Death and anything resembling awareness is absent.

Rather, ghouls are likely manipulated by forces the way dummy puppets are manipulated on strings. The Phantom of O'Donnell Heights qualifies under this definition, as do other creatures we will introduce to you in this book, for it was clearly an evildoer and evidently not of this world. His home was the graveyard.

Some people might feel that enigmas like the strange Phantom of O'Donnell Heights are humans cross-bred with other creatures; in other words, *humanoids* — creatures that are not humans, ghosts, ghouls, or monsters, but something other. Like the Phantom of O'Donnell Heights, humanoids possess human attributes, but are not humans. Extraterrestrials from other planets, such as Men in Black and Nordics, are often described by witnesses as resembling humans, while not being quite human.

"When I think of a ghoul, I think of those dead people in the movie *The Night of the Living Dead* and also in Michael Jackson's 'Thriller' video," said Diane Hill, my partner and best friend in the world, who fundamentally disagrees with any other definition.

Diane looked over at me from the other side of a weathered cedar picnic table in the tranquil greenery of the triangle park on Route 25 in Southold where we do much of our brainstorming and arguing over Sunday coffee. "When I think of a monster," she went on, "I think of a big old hairy thing with claws, like Sasquatch." She paused to consider a thought. "Oh, yes, and Frankenstein is a monster, too!"

Some people call creatures whose existence can't be confirmed "cryptids." In actuality, cryptids could be unknown species of animals or animals believed to be extinct. At best, we can only guess what these mysterious winged creatures of the night are and where they come from, for they don't lend themselves to being interviewed or having conversations wherein they explain themselves.

There's the case of the frogman of Coney Island that serves as a good example of a humanoid that is also a cryptid. The *New York Times* reported hundreds of people witnessed a man with wings and frog legs flying and swimming across the sky over Coney Island on a bright September day in 1880. I repeat: flying and swimming at the same time. He was about a thousand feet up in the air. The people on the ground reported that they could see the creature's face and they claimed it was clearly a man's face. He looked angry, determined. During that period of time the same being, or one just like it, was said to have been seen in other states, including Kentucky.

Only three years earlier, in September 1877, a winged human being was seen flying over Brooklyn, but few details from that sighting survived.

Was the frogman of Coney Island a ghost, a ghoul, or a monster? *Webster's Dictionary* tells us a monster "is part animal and part human in form, as a centaur, or made up of parts of two or more different animals..."

We know humans can't fly, so the frogman of Coney Island must have been something other than a human. The frogman was "part human in form," so according to the dictionary definition, the frogman was a monster. Simple!

The Jersey Devil, on the other hand, *is* a creature that people claim has the head of a horse with horns. Its front legs are short like those of a kangaroo's, but dangerously appointed with long, sharp, knife-like claws. This brown and black Devil stands on two hoofs and has a long, forked tail — like the tail of the Devil in Medieval and Renaissance paintings. People who have seen this creature say it's furry and as tall as a man.

Supposedly, the Jersey Devil has been stalking people and killing livestock in the Pinelands of New Jersey since 1735. The Pinelands cover one-third of the state. The hungry creature's range is far and wide, believed to extend into Pennsylvania. Napoleon Bonaparte's brother, Joseph Bonaparte, claimed to have actually seen this creature while hunting in Bordertown, New Jersey, around 1820.

Supposedly, in the late 1700s the Jersey Devil was shot by a canon ball, but kept flying.

More than 2,000 people have reportedly either seen the Jersey Devil or in some way been directly affected by its killing and ransacking. In January 1909, more than one hundred people reportedly saw the creature during a five-day period; and then supposedly, on January 21st of that year, men at the fire department in West Collingswood sprayed the Devil with a fire hose as it swooped down from the sky at them.

People who have claimed to seen the creature up close say it is a frightful sight. It has yellow-green eyes that sometimes also burn red. Its enormous wings are those of a giant bat's. Supposedly, a park ranger in Wharton State Forest in New Jersey came face-to-face with the infamous beast and said it stood on two legs like a human, six feet tall or so, and had black fur that was wet and matted. The creature's eyes were red, he said. It stared through the windshield of his vehicle at him.

The Jersey Devil is known to have maliciously swooped down over people in New Jersey's towns, perhaps looking for a child to snatch for a meal. This is a trait of a ghoul according to Arabic folklore: eating children.

There are folks who say that local people who have gone missing and were never heard from again were the victims of this awful being, which seems to like hiding out by creeks.

Is the Jersey Devil a ghost, ghoul, or monster? As far as we know, ghosts don't eat chickens, so we have to rule out the Jersey Devil being a ghost, which leaves the Devil to the classification of a ghoul or monster… We'll have to go with the Jersey Devil being a monster.

For readers who might feel these classifications are too limited and don't actually apply, then the term "other" might be more appropriate, as in not a ghost, not a ghoul, not a monster, but an "other." What does other mean?

There is no visual image that goes with "other" while the terms "ghoul" and "monster" conjure images we can readily envision, albeit inspired by Hollywood. For the purpose of this book, we are going to call the Jersey Devil a monster because it appears to be composed of parts from different animals.

However, I must say in my own mind, a strange, elusive, and hardly-ever-seen creature that stalks the woods and has the potential to kill humans for food is a true monster. The Jersey Devil qualifies as a monster under my personal definition, then, too.

An all-black being in a cape and hood, like the Phantom of O'Donnell Heights, and also something like the Jersey Devil in its stealth and ability to disappear back to some other world, allegedly appeared in a tree in Farmingdale in 2008. The creature is said to have long, bony, black fingers and thin arms. It stands about six-feet tall and weighs an estimated ninety pounds.

This alleged monster reportedly pointed its index finger at unsuspecting people having a springtime party in a backyard behind a fence bordering a quiet residential street in Farmingdale. It appeared to have five digits, indicating it was of the primate family, but what monkey or ape wears a cape and a hood? Was it part human? Was it part ape and part human…a monster?

We now call this monster "The Long Island Devil." A man walking his dog claimed to have seen the alleged entity. He claimed his dog looked up at the creature and watched it in disbelief, too.

The man said he and his dog observed the being for about two minutes and then the creature disappeared before their eyes. The witness said it turned into particles and simply vanished... Primates can't do that. In fact, no animal can do that!

The same being allegedly showed up again a year later outside a string of known haunted cemeteries in Farmingdale. The three graveyards are collectively referred to by ghost enthusiasts as the Old Quaker Burying Ground. The same man who saw the black being the first time, Patrick Kenney of Farmingdale, allegedly saw it this second time, too.

Kenney told us he spotted the entity standing on the street outside Powell Cemetery. Powell is a lovely treed family cemetery at the eastern end of the three cemeteries of the Old Quaker Burying Ground. After a few seconds, the creature vanished, Mr. Kenney claimed. He said his father saw the being, too, in yet a third sighting, when he, too, was walking the dog alone. However, we are told that the elder Mr. Kenney is not interested in discussing what he saw.

Is the younger Mr. Kenney crazy? Is his story of the creature in the tree ridiculous?

If so, then the husband and wife who have stories of a black being in their backyard in nearby Bethpage must also be crazy. Like Mr. Kenney's father, these folks are too private to come forward publicly with their creature sightings. They are not interested in speaking with us and we don't know their names. Instead, their stories were related to Diane and I and members of our audience at a library lecture we gave as The Paranormal Adventurers by a woman who said she knows the couple who saw it. She spoke about the couple's experiences during our lecture at Farmingdale Public Library in the spring of 2011.

It was no surprise to us that people in the area are seeing this alleged entity. Even before the woman told us about the couple, we had heard rumors of such sightings.

Dee-Dee Phillips of Dix Hills and Ashley Pappas of Farmingdale, who teach horseback riding at Bethpage Stables in Bethpage State Park, said they actually photographed a black being with red eyes in the woods at night with a cell phone in October 2010. The stables are not far from the graveyards.

We sat with these brave investigators at a table in an office at the stables one evening and went over the photos Ashley took of the black being. Stretched between two trees is the clear shape of a black form with its wings outstretched. This may have been the same black being that showed up in a photograph they took of a long breezeway in the stable where they sensed a presence. In this second photo, a black form blocks part of a wall at the end of the walkway.

Paranormal Investigator Dee-Dee Phillips. Through photography, Ouija Board, and EVP sessions, Dee-Dee and some of her associates at the Bethpage Stables in Bethpage State Park have contacted spiritual entities including "Za-Za." Dee-Dee and Ashley Pappas believe they caught the image of a black being with red eyes that appeared at night in the woods near a riding trail.

Ashley Pappas and Dee-Dee Phillips exploring the area in Bethpage State Park, where, on a night in October 2010, Ashley photographed a black figure between two trees.

"Being here at night I heard things, like talking and stuff," said Ashley. "One night I was down here by myself and I heard three or four different women talking. I looked around, but there was nobody there. So I called Dee and I said, 'Listen, I was in the barn and I heard some talking.' Dee asked exactly where I was when I heard it. I told her and she said, 'I heard some talking there the other day, too! It was women, right?' I said 'yeah, that's right!'"

In yet other photos Ashley took, the investigators feel they caught a pair of red eyes staring back at the camera. In one of these photos, the eyes appear to be staring down from a tree. "When I saw that shot, the first thing that came to my mind was *The Mothman Prophecies*," said Dee-Dee, referring to John A. Keel's book in which Keel investigates a black creature called Mothman that appeared to people over the course of a year in Point Pleasant, West Virginia. "My feeling is the thing in the photograph is not human."

Witnesses of the alleged black entity in the Farmingdale-Bethpage area, which we call the Long Island Devil, typically don't wish to speak publicly or even privately about their sightings for fear that they will be dragged into a circus-like public arena where their good names and reputations will be tarnished. They are afraid people will think they are nuts; and let's be realistic, they do have their jobs and the welfare of their children to worry about.

Diane and I can appreciate their feelings. In 2010, we were in one of the cemeteries of the Old Quaker Burying Ground in Farmingdale, searching for signs of the Long Island Devil, when we had our own unexpected experience: Something large and black jumped off a thick utility wire about thirty feet up in the air and flew right past me and was gone.

It happened so quickly... I only glimpsed it out of the corner of my eye, so I can't give a description. It moved too fast — incredibly fast. The only thing I can say about it was that I heard its wings beat once, or maybe it was the fluff of its cape, as it soared past me, but I'm not sure which.

Like the Bethpage couple, Mr. Kenney's father, and possibly other witnesses who are afraid to come forward, I wouldn't expect anybody to believe my story, either. However, lucky for me, I was holding a video camera at the time, which I turned on only seconds after the long black thing flew past me, and I recorded my story.

The video shows the thick, heavy utility wire still bouncing from the amazing force of the thing that jumped off it. The video of the "Incredible

Bouncing Wire" is on our website for viewing. You will quickly see that there was no way Diane nor I could have made that weighty wire bounce. Surely, the entire span of the wire from one utility pole to the other has to weigh many hundreds of pounds and is at least thirty feet off the ground, so there is no way we could have manipulated it. Several minutes passed before the incredible bouncing wire finally came to a rest.

Obviously, it is our opinion that something mysterious is going on in the Farmingdale-Bethpage area. The question we're left wondering is: How many other people have seen this alleged creature and not yet told anybody about it?

Is the Long Island Devil a ghost, ghoul, or monster? By dictionary definition, we would have to classify it as a monster because it seems to be part primate and part something else. However, according to the talented psychics who have investigated with us, the Long Island Devil hides out in cemeteries and thus possesses that same familiar graveyard attribute of the ghoul that we touched upon earlier when we discussed the Phantom of O'Donnell Heights, a creature that fled back to Death — and the graveyard from whence it came — when humans got too close.

Mount Misery and Sweet Hollow Road in Melville are places known for ghosts, ghouls, and monsters. This is not too surprising since Melville borders Farmingdale in an area just to the east of Bethpage State Park near the place where Patrick Kenney claimed to have seen the Long Island Devil. Farmingdale, we suspect, is either the place the alleged Devil dwells or passes through on its way to some other destination.

Some of the stories of Mount Misery and Sweet Hollow Road that circulate, such as the man who is seen from time to time darting though the edge of the woods at night on Mount Misery Road while carrying a bucketful of freshly severed heads, or the cop who stops vehicles in the middle of the night on Sweet Hollow Road only to reveal that the back of his head is missing, are outlandish, of course, and are easily dismissible because they are silly and easy to spot as false. However, stories of ghouls and monsters dwelling in the woods, and seen and heard at night, might have much more validity.

We are told that in 1969 a woman named Jaye P. Paro, a reporter and WBAB radio talk show personality, photographed a being in shabby black rags or matted black hair while she and two friends were in the woods of Mount Misery in broad daylight. The photograph, accompanied by an article Paro wrote, was subsequently published in *Beyond* magazine. Miss Paro's story was also recounted by John A. Keel, the famous investigator and author of *The Mothman Prophecies* (1975), in will? Are they invisible and among us without us even knowing they are there? Are they extraterrestrials?

Stop and think about Long Island's location on the globe: We are on an island jutting far out into the Atlantic Ocean from where mysterious life forms from the sea and air could take refuge, possibly in our woods.

Take the case of Diana Beller, 23, of Shirley, who said she saw a most peculiar bird one night in 2009 while driving home on the William Floyd Parkway, a north-south road that runs across Long Island and unofficially starts at the "east end."

Diana saw a strange "really round bird with a short neck" that stood about three feet tall running on the road. It was nighttime and the bird appeared in headlights strangely dodging speeding traffic.

"It was the strangest thing," Diana remembered. "It had big eyes and its eyes were really bugged out. It was scared. It had long legs and ran very fast. But it's strange," she paused, "its legs were fleshy. So were its head and neck. It had no feathers on its head. No feathers on its neck or legs. It could run very fast on these fleshy legs, this round bird. It definitely was a bird, but it wasn't a bird I've ever seen before. It wasn't a wild turkey. I've seen hundreds of them. I know what turkeys look like. I've seen blue herons and egrets and lots of other birds in Florida. They all have sleek bodies, but I never seen any bird like this on Long Island. I don't know what it was!"

Diana and I looked through a Peterson First Guides, *Birds: A Simplified Guide to the Common Birds of North America*, a bird book with pictures. We tried to identify the creature she saw on the road that night. We couldn't find a picture of such a bird in the book.

There's also the case of Carmela Somma of Manorville, who, before her tragic death, owned a large piece of woods in the Pine Barrens and considered herself an observant bird watcher. One day, kindly, white-haired Mrs. Somma found herself alone in her yard when a flock of "very large" black birds descended from the blue sky like the wicked witch's army of flying monkeys in *The Wizard of Oz*. The birds overtook the towering trees in the three wooded acres of her backyard and screamed at her as she gazed up at them, terrified.

"I was scared," recalled Mrs. Somma. "They were nearly as big as me! I ran inside the house. These birds were nothing like ravens, they were much, much larger and hulky. Their feathers were not neatly aligned. The feathers were fluffed like these birds just finished swimming, but they didn't have webbed feet, and they weren't wet — it's just how their

Anoth
was seen
it 'horrib
Cryptozool
its body a
been big,
creature a
assailant \
face and r
like a giar

Could
tribes fro
it darkenc
Creatures f
reports o
southwest
and very
is suppos
dining on
to get awz
thundero

There
list, but n
other pla
home, Lo
as the Lo
right now

While
question,
you to cc
greatest p
and being
look for
get there

Many
stories th
tell these
Island or
seen one
include t

feathers looked all the time, I guess. These birds were frightening-looking, like monsters. I was afraid they'd swoop down and get me! I never saw anything like them before!"

Mrs. Somma and I sat at her kitchen table and turned the pages of the same Peterson's Birds book I explored with Diana Beller, but we found no pictures of birds that matched the birds she saw.

In both Carmela Somma's and Diana Beller's cases, the birds could have been migrating birds that stopped off in Long Island to eat and rest before continuing their long, hard flights to some other places.

Certainly, unusual birds that may not be shown in pictures in *Birds: A Simplified Guide to the Common Birds of North America* may visit Long Island. For example, a snowy owl from the arctic was photographed one summer on the boardwalk of Long Beach on the south shore of Nassau County in the 1990s. Its picture appeared on the front page of the *Long Beach Herald*, of which I was a reporter for at the time, but a picture of a snowy owl is not presented in Peterson's *Birds: A Simplified Guide to the Common Birds of North America* because it is not a bird that is commonly seen in the populated areas of North America, but much farther north, in the arctic. So, assuredly, creatures from other places that are not native to Long Island do sometimes visit Long Island — and this is true with animals from the sea, too.

Though it may not be common, schools of large fish sometimes lose their way in the Atlantic and find themselves jumping for smaller fish in the Long Island Sound and in the harbors of the north shore. Many experienced fishermen will rush to Cedar Beach in Mount Sinai, for example, when jumping tuna, known as "false albacore," stray into the Sound, eat small fish along the shoreline, and clamber into the salt marsh of the harbor for a meal of lobsters, crabs, clams, and small school fish.

Whales and sharks are also known to stray into Long Island's waters. Though enormous blue whales are not commonly seen, a juvenile stranded itself on the beach of East Hampton in Suffolk County in 2010 with grave results. Great white sharks have been caught off Montauk Point, too, though they are rarely seen in local waters and are much more likely to be found in warmer waters such as those off Australia's coast. But what about more exotic animals of the sea? Could strange forms of life swim up and out of the breakers, climb out of the wet sand, and drag themselves to our local woods?

An article about strange creatures from the sea appeared in a 2010 issue of *Science Illustrated*. The article, "The Beasts Below: Into the Abyss," reported that only five percent of the Earth's oceans have been explored.

The
wond
deep
surfa
ones
cold
of lif
Islan

I
and
inves
some
creat

S
that
Repo
gent
like
have
alley
the g
that

S
Heig
outs
Islan

to be
in E
agai
brov

Mar
sittir
The
to h
witn
tree
have
who

Section One:
Ghosts

The Lonely
Ship Captain's Ghost

LOCATION: Port Jefferson

DIRECTIONS: Take the Long Island Expressway to Exit 64 north (Route 112). Drive all the way north till you reach Port Jefferson Harbor on the Long Island Sound. Once in Port Jefferson Village, signs will direct you to the Ferry.

A Sea Captain Pines for Earlier Days

Two people have reported seeing the ghost of a weathered ship's captain aboard the Port Jefferson Ferry as it crossed the Long Island Sound from Bridgeport, Connecticut, to Port Jefferson, Long Island, some years back.

Ship captains are a noble lot, and if an important captain of an important boat, such as the ferry, should appear as a ghost, surely he would be the ghost of a man of strength and integrity, just like the ghost of the man we are about to discuss, according to witnesses.

One of the witnesses — a man who claimed to be a former worker aboard one of the Port Jefferson Steamboat Company's boats (the *P. T. Barnum*, *Grand Republic*, and *Park City*) — would only tell us his story if we promised not to reveal his name or when he worked for the 129-year-old company.

"It was a ghost that I saw, alright," said the man, rubbing his gray whiskers, thinking back to when he was a younger man. "There's no doubt about that. It still gives me the willies, but it was kind of cool, too, you know?"

The following is his account:

"What happened was we left Bridgeport, Connecticut, at eight o'clock in the evening," recalled the former crew member, beginning his unbelievable story. "It was the last trip of the day. The October night was windy and cold, and no boats were traveling out on the rough water.

The *Grand Republic*, one of the ferries that operates between Port Jefferson and Bridgeport, Connecticut. At least two people allege to have seen the ghost of a lonely ship's captain at different times aboard ferries returning from Connecticut during evening storms. Have you seen the ghost of the nostalgic captain?

"I remember the swells were high when it started lightning. We didn't have many vehicles aboard that evening going to Long Island, so I guess not many people wanted to travel in that god-awful weather. I was looking forward to getting home to Port Jeff to have some hot clam chowder and a steaming cup of hot coffee at the village tavern where we sailors sometimes gather on cold nights and swap stories.

"Well, as it was, I was astern sweeping around the chairs and benches on back of the main deck, like I did every night, you know, cigarette butts and soda cans, when all of a sudden I see this guy standing by himself against the back rail. He's looking all sad sort of back at Bridgeport. We were nearing Port Jefferson by this time. The thing of it was, he hadn't been there a second or two ago. Nobody was. He just popped onto the boat from out of nowhere!

"So, I hold still and steady myself by holding onto the outside bar and I look at this strange man because he's got my attention now, you see, standing there as he was, an old guy with white hair, wearing a sailor's dark pea coat with the tall collar up at the sides of his rough neck. He had a neat white beard and a black and white captain's hat on his head. He had his big hands in the pockets of the dark blue pea coat. I thought he looked like the statues of 'The Captain' that you see in so many Long Island and New England homes. I figured him for the captain of a whaling vessel, or maybe a fishing boat, or maybe even a tugboat like them McAllister boats back in Port Jefferson.

"Anyway, this captain guy stood strong in the wind like the gusts and the pelting rain and cracking lightning didn't even bother him none. He was a salty old sailor for sure. Then he pulled out a black pipe from his pocket and stuck it in his mouth. I knew I was looking at the image of what a man is supposed to be – strong, brave, you know, not afraid of what might come – but I sensed he was sad. Oh, yes, sad.

The maritime man paused before continuing on with his story.

"I tried to see his face... He was looking back at Bridgeport and the long trail that the boat's propeller cut in the black water, like a foamy highway back to Connecticut. I thought at the time that maybe he missed somebody who he left back there. Maybe he missed his wife and the smell of her hair, or his family, or the ship he once captained. I felt bad for him. He looked so sad. I think he had a regret or two inside his heart.

"Then, all at once I turn in such a way that I could see the green light of a buoy right through him! Jesus, Mary, and Joseph! With that a lightning bolt strikes across the sky and into the distant waters. Then a crack of thunder ripped across the heavens like Jesus coming back at the second coming!

"He quickly turned all shadowy and wispy like pipe smoke and I could see the white caps of the furious water right through him as I got closer. Then he turns around and he was all aglow and white. I couldn't make out the details of his face any more because a fog was blowing in and covering him suddenly in a blanket of thick white mist. I could only sense that he was looking past me. Then he nods in such a way that I thought he was giving an Okay to somebody who wasn't there, so I looked around, but no one was there! Then, when I turned back, I see him up and just vanish like smoke into the wind! Just like that!"

For some people, the one hour and fifteen-minute ferry ride from Bridgeport, Connecticut, to Long Island is a bit more than they paid for, but worth the trip, they say.

"Sally," a Miller Place resident who was returning to Long Island from visiting her daughter and three grandchildren in Boston, Massachusetts, saw the ghost of the sea captain at port side of the boat as she was returning home on the late ferry. Again, lightning was flashing in the sky in sudden jagged blue bolts and cracking overhead were thunder claps that sounded like atomic bombs exploding.

The following is Sally's recollection of seeing this portly ghost:

"The boat wasn't crowded, so I had a booth all to myself inside the warm cabin. I had been reading a book about a woman who found the man of her dreams, but that's not important. What's important was that my attention was drawn out the window to a man who appeared there from out of nowhere. He was a handsome gentleman with a sailor's cap on his white head, a dark sailor's jacket on his strong chest. I didn't see a wedding ring. I could see he had a white beard, too. I couldn't see his face except when he turned to the left. He was mostly standing still and looking out over the passing water at the side of the boat.

"I thought to myself, isn't that strange? A handsome man, alone, is standing out in the cold of the late November night without so much as flinching at the hard winds? It was lightning out. What possessed him to remain out there? I didn't know!

"It was an awful night. The boat rocked a little because the waves were high, but this gentleman stood his ground on the deck without so much as grabbing onto the handrail. I thought, 'Well, I never!'

"I put my book down – I was on page 211, I remember – and watched this fellow for a minute because there was something peculiar about him. He seemed lifeless. I soon noticed he was standing still and not even moving with the boat. 'This is unnatural!' I said to myself. I looked around to see who else saw this man, but everyone was having fun talking or reading or sipping coffee or hot chocolate, so I cupped my hands around my face at the window to escape the light of the cabin and took a closer look at him outside in the dark night. It was at this point that he bowed his head and turned to the side so that I could see his face. This time he had no eyes!

"No sooner had I realized this when suddenly he transformed into a white vapor, a mist, and was nowhere to be seen!

"At first I thought maybe I should go out and check to see if there was such a passenger aboard the ship, but I knew he wasn't real. I knew I had just seen a ghost. I looked out at the fog that was shrouding the boat now and I vowed to myself that I wouldn't dare tell a soul because they would think I had been drinking or that I was nuts!

"I waited in the parking lot at Port Jefferson just the same to see if I could recognize anyone resembling this man getting off the boat. My Jaguar was one of the first cars off the ferry, so I pulled over at a place where I had a clear view of the drivers as they got off the boat in their cars and pulled away to go home. Nobody looked anything like this man!

"'Sally,' I said to myself. 'Girl, you have just seen a ghost!' And a good-looking single man he was! Now, when I'm coming home from Boston, I always take the eight o'clock ferry so that maybe I can see him again. I think he must only appear in storms because that's the only time I saw him. It's been years. So far, I haven't had any luck. But I'm still looking. I know he's out there – somewhere! They don't make them like that anymore. A real man!"

Since interviewing these witnesses — the crew member and passenger — we have taken the Port Jefferson Ferry on several occasions. However, we have never encountered the ghost of the lonely old ship's captain.

Meanwhile, many telephone calls placed in the spring and summer of 2011 to the Port Jefferson Ferry Company for a spokesperson's comment about the alleged ghost of the sea captain went unreturned.

Will the captain ever be seen again?

The Fighting Spirits
at the Fire Island Lighthouse

LOCATION: Fire Island National Seashore

DIRECTIONS: The lighthouse is at the western end of the Fire Island National Seashore, just east of Robert Moses State Park. Take Robert Moses Causeway south to the end. At the Robert Moses Water Tower, proceed east to parking field #5. There is a parking fee at certain times of the year. Park on the east side of the parking field and follow the boardwalk to the lighthouse.

CONTACT INFORMATION: 631-661-4876

WEBSITES: Fire Island Lighthouse Historical Society: *www.fireislandlighthouse.com*; National Park Service: *www.nps.gov/fiis*

Did ghosts once dwell in the Fire Island Lighthouse? Do they still?

Painting of the Fire Island Lighthouse by Claire Reese, 1948,
and the lighthouse present day, viewed from different angles.

The Ghosts of Fire Island

Whistling Sam

There are many ghost stories about Fire Island.

For twenty-two years, Richard Barrett was an officer with the Suffolk County Police Marine Bureau. After retiring from there, he went on to become a National Park Service Law Enforcement Ranger for seventeen years, during which he patrolled Fire Island. Every year since Barrett has been telling a whopper of a story about the ghost of Whistling Sam.

However, if you want to know more about Whistling Sam's ghost, you will have to see Barrett speak into a microphone at night in front of the Fire Island Lighthouse sometime around Halloween. Hundreds of people brave the cold and wind for this uniquely Long Island annual event.

Barrett is probably more knowledgeable than almost anyone else about the strange occurrences that take place in the middle of the night on Fire Island. He stands in a pool of light against the towering black and white lighthouse, 168 feet tall, while hundreds of people listen to his ghost stories. They are snuggled in blankets and sitting on the hard ground of the huge stone terrace or in fold-up chairs they brought along with them. Many parents have children on their laps. When Barrett talks about Whistling Sam's ghost, even the children seem to quiet down and sit a little stiller.

Barrett is a kindly white-haired gentleman who wears glasses and boasts a thick white mustache. He looks as strong as a grizzly bear and has a bit of the tough, no-nonsense New York cop about him. He wears a black cowboy hat and a blue down jacket against the cold autumn winds blowing in from off the raw Atlantic Ocean. He smiles gently, summoning confidence in him and a friendliness from him. His strength is like the Fire Island Lighthouse itself, pure Long Island, tall and sturdy.

What we will reveal to you right now about Whistling Sam is that when he was alive he was an African American cook aboard a schooner that shipwrecked off Fire Island. Now Sam is a ghost.

Will you hear Sam whistling the next time you're in the Fire Island dunes? Will you see him walking on the beach?

It's a good story. Next Halloween season go to the Fire Island Lighthouse and hear Barrett tell the story for yourself.

Richard Barrett tells ghost stories at the Fire Island Lighthouse every year during Halloween season. Nobody knows better what stirs on Fire Island in the night than Mr. Barrett, the story-teller and bearer of secrets about the ghost of Whistling Sam.

The Haunting Ghost

There's a ghost story that was told in a novel published many years back, the name of which I have forgotten. I tried to look it up in the library and on Amazon, but couldn't find it. It was about a ghost that caused a traffic accident on the West Side Highway in Manhattan and almost killed the poor driver. This happened after the ghost had haunted the man and other people to near distraction on Fire Island for some time. The ghost followed the driver into Manhattan.

The author of this Fire Island ghost story said the story was a true account — no doubt indulged here and there — but true, nonetheless. That novel scared me when I read it in the 1980s. Back then I didn't know that ghosts sometimes tried to kill people. Twenty years later, Diane and I would fly to Nashville, Tennessee, and then drive north to Adams, near the Kentucky border, to investigate the Bell Witch Ghost on John Bell's former farm. The state of Tennessee recognizes a spirit as the killer of John Bell in 1820. There's a bronze plaque outside the old brick Bell Schoolhouse telling the story. It's the only known case on record of a ghost actually killing a human. It's extremely rare that spirits hurt people. John Bell was poisoned by the ghost known as The Bell Witch after she administered a black liquid to John Bell as he lay near death in bed. The same stuff killed the family cat when it was fed the poisonous black liquid. To this day, it's common to see dead cats in the streets and on country roads around Adams, Tennessee. We don't know if it's a coincidence or if the Bell Witch just has a mean sense of humor. Some people believe the entity still dwells in Adams. Diane and I would have to agree.

We don't know whatever became of that ghost and the haunted man who was in the car accident on the West Side Highway. The novel was a good read, however. It ended with the man going on television and telling his story of the ghost of Fire Island on a national talk show. The author made it a big point to indicate his appearance on a talk show was true. He didn't reveal what show it was, exactly; I kind of got the feeling that the host was a big wheel in the television business, which means that the man had the nation's attention with his ghost story.

A scary ghost story, for sure.

The Dead Sea Captain

There's the ghost story about Captain William H. Squires from Good Ground, now called Hampton Bays. Squires' dead body floated thirty miles east along the shore of Fire Island and Long Island — going against the strong Atlantic current — to return home to Good Ground, the place of his residence. Legends say his frozen body washed-up only yards from his home so his family could find him and bury him properly. This occurred thirteen days after his ship wrecked and he died. Good Ground was the same town where he was born and where much of his family lived, died, and was also buried.

Due to his ghostly efforts to return home, Good Ground, or Hampton Bays, would be the place where this captain of the *Louis V. Place* shipwreck would be buried, too.

Today there are many graves belonging to the Squires family that can be found in Good Cemetery in Hampton Bays. These graves are situated in close proximity to the back of the United Methodist Church on Main Street.

Grave of Captain William H. Squires, who froze to death on the shipwrecked *Louis V. Place* in 1895. His frozen body fell into the stormy ocean and drifted thirty miles against the current to find its way home to Hampton Bays, then called Good Ground.

The ghost story of Captain Squires' is a true Long Island ghost story through and through. William H. Squires was a hardy sea captain from a noteworthy Long Island family, who, along with some of his men, tried to escape the torturous icy waves smacking the life out of his wrecked ship, the spray from which immediately turned to ice on their faces and clothing. The exhausted men climbed high up into the rope rigging hanging from the ship's tall masts.

Captain Squires was no lily-livered landlubber, for he was a descendent of Ellis Squires, who supposedly rowed a clumsy whale boat down to Long Island from Maine in 1640 with his wife and their nine kids clutching for their lives inside the boat. The story sounds like fiction, but supposedly it's true.

Opposite Page: Retouched photograph of the battered *Louis V. Place*. The doomed three-masted schooner struck a sandbar off Fire Island across from Sayville. **Above:** Retouched photograph of a frozen man hanging dead in the rigging of the ship. It was from the rigging that Captain William H. Squires fell into the icy Atlantic and was carried home against the current. Many people who saw the ship on the sandbar said they saw the ghost of Captain Squires in the lower rigging. This same image was captured in a photograph titled "Ghost in the Rigging," which is on display at the Long Island Maritime Museum in West Sayville. *Photographs courtesy of the Long Island Maritime Museum.*

Ellis Squires was the first white man to settle the area that is today called Hampton Bays. His whaleboat first touched land at Southampton and then Ellis rowed the whaleboat inland to a place that is today called Red Creek. The area where the Squires family settled is still known as Squiretown. At one time it was an artists' community. Many members of the Squires family still live in the area.

With such a family history, it might be suggested that William H. Squires was born to be a ship's captain; after all, it was in his genes, his legacy, his destiny.

However, being a descendent in a noble bloodline of brave sea captains did not protect William H. Squires from the blasts of Neptune's tempestuous fury. Like some of the other sailors on the ship, eventually, the good captain froze to death and fell like a white log from the iced rigging of the *Louis V. Place*, a three-masted schooner, into the smashing waters of the frigid black Atlantic. For Patchogue Villagers at the time, this was a particularly memorable event. Some of the sailors who died in this tragedy were buried in Lakeview Cemetery in Patchogue Village. This happened just prior to the graveyard erupting with a ghost. The ghost became so famous newspaper articles were written about it, but *that's* another story.

Days earlier, the sails of Captain Squires' ship had frozen to the stiffness of oak boards in the pelting whiteout snowstorm as the *Louis V. Place* fought its way out of Baltimore, Maryland. The creaking cargo area of the ship was laden with 1,100 tons of precious black coal bound for New York. The sailors lost control of the mighty sails because ice built up thickly on the canvases. The ship was rendered unmanageable, going where it would in the ungodly frozen and ferocious winds, eventually smacking right into a sandbar off Fire Island, a dead-zone for sailors, a place from which it was unlikely to ever return.

Call it Captain Squires' fate.

Two days passed before rescuers could get to the battered brown ship covered in pewter ice and crystal white snow, stuck as it was in the relentlessly pounding waves on the hopelessly tragic sandbar. The ship had broken apart like Captain Squires' future. Rescuers from the Long Island Life Saving Service on Lone Hill on Fire Island, the predecessor of the U.S. Coast Guard, were repelled by the fierce ocean that roared like an angry lion in their bruised faces. Wind gusts blew upwards of seventy miles an hour while the temperature hovered around two degrees. It was a terrible storm. No man could quell its might. It claimed other ships along the southern beaches of Long Island, as well. This storm would be cursed by sailors for many years to come.

When it was all over and the good fight was finished, the ghost of Captain William H. Squires managed to somehow get his body home to be buried with other members of his proud lineage. No small accomplishment.

Authors' Note: The previous three examples of Fire Island ghost stories are all good to tell around a campfire. Like many ghost stories, they might or might not be completely true. For now, though, let's put these stories aside. It's time for us to introduce a new and true Fire Island ghost story.

The Ghosts of Fire Island II

By the time Diane and I started investigating the Fire Island Lighthouse, it had reputedly been haunted for many decades. There were dark stories of a suicide by a lightkeeper and of children dying. There were tales about ghosts haunting the ominously tall and imposing structure. Some people said poltergeists could be spotted looking out windows at visitors milling about outside on the terrace. People claimed that if you listened intently at midnight, you could hear ghosts crying.

The Mahlers' former living quarters at the Fire Island Lighthouse from 1948 to 1954. The Mahlers are uniquely qualified to speak about the ghosts of the Fire Island Lighthouse.

However, none of these ghost stories ever held up to scrutiny when compared to the real facts. For example, nobody ever committed suicide in the lighthouse, especially not a keeper.

The spooky Fire Island Lighthouse ghost stories that had been circulating for years were always predicated upon one's ability to successfully suspend the truth in one's own mind. It's as if the creators of the legends many years back in time asked us to believe anything they told us just long enough for us to bite and swallow their ghost stories, but please do not digest them intellectually or compare them to the historical facts. That's just how many legends are — anti-intellectual.

Interviewing people who would know the truth of the stories would inevitably and invariably prove the ghost stories false. For example, the lighthouse guide who led Diane and me on a tour when we visited there with a group of ghost hunters vehemently denied the lighthouse was haunted, adding that he and his wife had been working at the lighthouse for fifteen years and they would know if it had ghosts.

Reportedly, a man hanged himself in the tower in the 1800s. Then, many years ago, when families lived in the lighthouse, the little girl

View facing east from the observation deck atop the Fire Island Lighthouse.

of a lighthouse keeper died of an illness that destroyed the keeper emotionally. Today the keeper's moans are said to be heard in the wee hours of the night inside the endlessly tall tower of 156 iron stairs and two ladders.

"I heard a lot of stories about the lighthouse being haunted," said our tour guide, "but I've never seen anything of that myself. I can't say what other people have or haven't seen."

From the top of the lighthouse, our tour guide looked down over the quilt-like patches of brown and green landscape below as the wind blew strong from off the vast blue Atlantic in the near distance, cold, deep, and angry, just a short walk away over the dunes. "I mean, there were plane crashes and other things here," he added, "but haunted? No... not that I have seen."

The plane crash piqued our curiosity. When questioned about it, the guide pointed down at the terrain immediately beside the lighthouse. "Yes, a plane crashed right there," he said.

It seems, then, that most of the stories we Long Islanders know about the ghosts of the Fire Island Lighthouse are just legends and tall tales, which have surfaced among the populace of Fire Island in whispers for many years — and for good reason: On Fire Island one can hear screams of ghosts from the ocean at night. The ghosts of shipwrecks call to people, some claim, but it's hard to separate the sounds of the wails and screams from the sounds of the surf. This had long been a problem when boats had gone missing in the area, for if people in trouble were screaming for help from a boat out beyond the breakers, their calls just blended into the surf and the dark night obliterating the endless, black mystical ocean. People who live on Fire Island say you just have to get used to the screaming and to asking yourself whether or not the screams you hear are just the surf, stranded sailors, or ghosts. In the end, who knows?

Thus, rumors of ghosts on Fire Island, and more specifically, the Fire Island Lighthouse, have taken on a life of their own and become the truth, despite the fact that they are chiefly false. Again, that's how legends work — they are like playing a telephone game whereby a message is passed from one person to another and gets so screwed up by the end of the game that the last story is hardly recognizable as the original message. This is why the ghost story we are going to tell you now is so striking, for it is based on actual events experienced by one Mrs. Marilyn (Lynne) Mahler.

In 1948, Mr. Gottfried Mahler was appointed the head lighthouse keeper at the Fire Island Lighthouse, a United States Coast Guard position. As a result of this appointment, Mrs. Mahler, Mr. Mahler, and their three sons lived in the lighthouse for six years.

The experience Mrs. Mahler had with spirits while living in the lighthouse from 1948 to 1954 makes her uniquely qualified to speak about the ghosts of the Fire Island Lighthouse. Hers was the last family of lighthouse keepers to ever live in the lighthouse. The Mahlers are the champions of a romantic tradition from yesteryear that many Long Islanders and tourists to our island find quaint and charming.

Lighthouse keepers — men, women and their children — were a breed of sturdy folks who measured themselves against challenging hardships and the brutal forces of nature. They braved wild storms, the smashing surf, biting bugs, oppressive heat, and hard travel. Moreover, they were always at the ready to help people in trouble.

The need for lighthouse keepers has been pushed to the wayside thanks to improvements in technology. While technological advances are good, we can't help feel that we also lost something of our heritage when we lost lighthouse keepers.

And guess what? The lighthouse really is haunted. At least it was haunted at one time, says Mrs. Mahler.

The Mahlers told us their stories on two separate occasions when we visited them in their home in Bay Shore. We brought a video camera and a voice recorder to make sure we got every word.

Marilyn (Lynne) and Gottfried Mahler are shown on their wedding day in 1945 and, more recently, in 2010.

Fighting Spirits at the Fire Island Lighthouse

"It was like a bar brawl!" began Mrs. Mahler. The following is her account of the ghosts she say occupied the lighthouse at one time.

"I had experienced these weird noises. I'd say they started after six months that we were there.

"I didn't think too much of it... I thought the other keeper (assistant in a second apartment in the lighthouse) was making the noises, that they were moving something around."

Mrs. Mahler looked around her living room in the Mahlers' Bay Shore ranch as she recalled the story. There are many photographs and paintings of the lighthouse on the walls, many knickknacks and pictures that are beautiful remembrances of the family's amazingly adventurous time spent in the windy lighthouse, a place where, at night, gales howled like wolves and the stars shined brightly like diamonds in the black velvet heavens. She looked to her husband of sixty-six years as she recalled the story, as if seeing the night all over again in her mind's eye.

Try to picture the night for yourself:

Mr. Mahler, who Mrs. Mahler had married only three years earlier, was not home on the windswept island on this foggy night because he was called away to fulfill important duties for the Coast Guard related to the lighthouse; and the assistant lighthouse keeper and his family, who lived in a second apartment in the lighthouse, were also off the island for the night. So, Mrs. Mahler was alone with her young boys.

There were no bridges off Fire Island at the time. The Robert Moses Bridge and Causeway had not yet been built. People had to travel to and from Fire Island by boat, so it was not yet a popular place. There were no flat walkways or boardwalks, either, as there are today. The Mahlers had to trudge the goods they shipped in from stores in Bay Shore on the south shore of Long Island — seven miles across the Great South Bay — through the sand dunes from the boat and up to the lighthouse. Mr. Mahler related that this was particularly difficult with a freezer they brought with them to Fire Island when they first moved in. They did have electricity, however.

Later in their stay on the island, Mrs. Mahler bought and drove a Model A Ford fitted with oversized tires and an improved roof to travel the dunes to get around the island because she was not permitted to drive the government Jeep used by her husband. "It was my dune buggy," she recalled.

The room on the left side of the lighthouse's main entrance, which today is the gift shop, was the Mahlers' living room. On the right side of the entrance, symmetrically, was the assistant keeper's apartment. The bedrooms for both apartments were on the second floor. Between the apartments was a staircase going to the second floor, to an area not occupied by the apartments, but between the apartments.

The nearest humans were in Kismet, two miles away across the same dunes where it's said the ghost of Whistling Sam appears from the *other side*, and from where you can hear, if you really listen, screaming in the night beyond the breakers.

That's how it was on the lonely night when the noises of the spirits came to the Fire Island Lighthouse — that's what Mrs. Mahler's mind's eye saw as she recalled what happened that haunted night.

"It was always in the same place. If you stand and look up the staircase from the foyer, it was always up there, where you always heard these noises. They had a trap entrance up there going into the ceiling loft, so I didn't know whether a fellow was in there or not.

"So, when I closed my doors, I wouldn't see anything in the foyer because I was then isolated in my apartment.

"At night, after everybody's bedded down, I would do my sewing for the boys' summer outfits, their little shorts and tank tops. And I suddenly hear this noise.

"Well, I knew the keeper and his family were ashore, so we were the only ones in the house. Where is this noise coming from?

"And it was getting louder and louder...like a bar brawl, like they were fighting up there!

"Now, some tales that I heard on the beach said these fights were at one time very predominant in the lighthouse. And the drinking that went on! Oh, my!

"So, I say, well what is this now? So, I opened the door to the foyer, and I listened, and the noises stopped."

For a few seconds Mrs. Mahler pauses in her story to revisit her mind's eye and see the exact moment she guardedly leaned into the open area of the foyer from her apartment door and looked up the tall, dark staircase going to the second floor. Today on the second floor there are exhibits and displays for visitors to view; the lighthouse is a museum maintained by Fire Island Lighthouse Preservation Society.

Staircase leading to the second floor from the foyer in the Fire Island Lighthouse. The ghostly noises Mrs. Mahler heard when she was alone with the children at night came from a loft in the ceiling at the top of the stairs. Were the noises ghosts fighting?

On that night back then, though, with a cold Atlantic fog blowing in off the breakers and wrapping itself like a snake around the lighthouse, the wind howling like wolves, an occasional foghorn sounding mournful in the mysterious distance, the spinning light in the lighthouse tower illuminating the rolling mists, as Mrs. Mahler gazed up into the darkness into which the stairs vanished, she felt a pang of dread on account of being plagued by something from beyond the grave, from the paranormal, by ghosts. What could be up there making that noise? Why was this madness happening when her husband and the assistant lighthouse keeper were not at home?

Mrs. Mahler continued with her story: she closed the door, locked it, and stared for a moment into the rushing thoughts of her wild imagination.

"So, I went back to what I was doing again, then later, I went back out again to check for anything strange, but I didn't hear anything. There was nothing.

"When it got to be about midnight...I don't know why it occurred at that particular time, but the noises got very, very loud.

"So, I went out in the hall and shouted 'Go home! Just go home!'

"And that was it. They were gone... After I yelled at them, they were gone!"

The thing is Mrs. Mahler experienced these noises "five or six times." Only on the last night that the brawling spirit visitors created a raucous did she step out into the foyer and yell up the stairs for them to leave. She had to rely on herself on this night to protect her children and she was not the kind to fold up house and leave because of a handful of noisy ghosts. It would be the other way around — she'd kick them out!

The obvious question is could the noises have been caused by raccoons or other animals?

"No way," said Mr. Mahler. "Raccoons wouldn't be up there."

The Mahlers' son, Goff, who was present when we interviewed Mr. and Mrs. Mahler, jumped into the discussion to agree with his parents. "Not up there," he said. "There wouldn't be raccoons or other animals up there."

Later in our discussions, we speculated with the Mahlers whether or not the spirits who were stirring in the loft were those belonging to Coast Guardsmen. After all, at one time, fifty Coast Guardsmen were stationed in the lighthouse at the same time during World War II. They patrolled Fire Island's beaches for German submarines. Often there were fist-fights and crass drunkenness as the men struggled to live together, many of them crammed in with each other in the loft.

The 156 iron stairs inside the tower of the Fire Island Lighthouse.
Do ghosts walk these stairs at night?

Lighthouse Legends and Ghosts

According to Mrs. Mahler, the ghost stories of the Fire Island Lighthouse were always actually a sore point with folks from local hamlets on Fire Island. Ladies in Mrs. Mahler's sewing club — the "Knitwits," as they called themselves — would not visit the Mahlers' residence because of suspicions that there were ghosts inside.

Instead, the women met at every other woman's house to knit together and banter as a group. They would make sweaters for their children and gifts for Christmastime, other holidays, and special events.

Folks were afraid to enter the lighthouse to socialize with Mrs. Mahler and her family because of the strange tales they heard, which made them feel too uncomfortable to gather together in the imposing building — it was as if the lighthouse was a haunted house on a graveyard hill.

Though the Mahlers never saw a ghost while living there, Mrs. Mahler is sure she had a few with her on those nights she heard the fighting in the loft.

So was the Fire Island Lighthouse haunted?

"Yes," says Mrs. Mahler. "Yes, the Fire Island Lighthouse was definitely haunted. Whether it still is today, I don't know."

The Roadside Ghosts of Grumman Memorial Park

LOCATION: Intersection of Route 25A and
Route 25, Calverton

DIRECTIONS: Take the Long Island Expressway to Exit 69 (Wading River Road). Go north on Wading River Road to Route 25. Make a right onto Route 25 and continue past Calverton National Cemetery. Grumman Memorial Park will be on the right-hand side.

Are the ghosts people see walking on the road in front of Grumman Memorial Park in Calverton the ghosts of former Grumman employees?

Meeting Place for the
Ghosts of Deceased Employees?

Have you ever passed by Grumman Memorial Park in Calverton and seen ghosts? Yet ghosts are exactly what several people we interviewed saw at different times when they were driving by the park on the lonely stretch of Route 25 at night.

Long Island's Largest Employer

For most of its 64-year history, Grumman was the leading employer on Long Island. At its height in the mid-eighties, the aerospace giant employed 23,000 people and supplied the government with cutting-edge technology used by the military to defend the United States and its allies.

In 1994, Grumman ceased to exist when it was sold to Northrop. The incomes it provided to so many Long Islanders evaporated. The work that people counted on moved off Long Island, but did something else remain behind?

Mike, a Mastic resident, told us the following story after a lecture we gave at the Mastic-Moriches-Shirley Community Library in 2008:

"I was driving home late at night after I finished work.

"It's dark on the road I'm talking about. There are lots of deer in this area, but on this night I noticed some kind of commotion on the road ahead. I put my bright headlights on, thinking maybe there were some deer walking around on the road, but in the light I see all these people smiling and talking as they're walking along the shoulder. The thing is...I could see right through them!

"I thought, 'Holy smoke, what's that?' I didn't see any cars parked around, so where did all these people come from? Who are they? There must have been ten of them! Why are they walking on this dark road after midnight? I felt a shiver run up my spine because I knew it wasn't natural.

"As I passed, I tried to make out their faces, but they were blurry and sort of wavy...like flags in the wind.

This section of road in front of Grumman Memorial Park on Route 25 in Calverton is where people have seen groups of ghosts walking at night.

"After I passed I looked back and saw glimmers on the shoulder of the road like weird sparkles of light. So I slowed down. 'Where are the people I just saw?' I wondered. 'Where did they go? How could they just disappear?'

"There was nobody else on the road, so I stopped the car and searched for them in the rear-view mirror.

"As I watched, the sparkles I had seen just faded to nothing and there was nobody there! But when I passed the spot only seconds before I saw a large group of men and women! Man, was I was confused!

"So, I swung the car around and drove past that spot again. I'm not the kind who gives up easily. I figured I was going to get to the bottom of this, but when I drove past the spot, I saw nothing there. Nothing but the Grumman jets on display in that little park – right up the road from Calverton National Cemetery."

Mike looked concerned as he asked us: "Do you think they were the ghosts of people who once worked for Grumman and maybe were buried in Calverton National Cemetery when they died? Do you think maybe they like to go to that spot to remember the days when they worked together at Grumman and were happy?"

Nobody can say for sure what Mike saw, but his experience at Grumman Memorial Park is the only time he ever saw ghosts, he said. These days he drives slowly when he passes the park, hoping to catch another glimpse of the ghosts he saw in 2008.

Calverton National Cemetery

Mike was right about the cemetery up the road.

Calverton National Cemetery is a burial ground for men and women who served in the military and their spouses. The cemetery is 1,045 acres and well over 200,000 people have been buried there since 1978. Surely, some of these people might have worked for Grumman or its subcontractors.

If there are ghosts that meet at Grumman Memorial Park nightly, it very well might explain what happened to Donna when she drove past the park one night in 2010.

Donna, a Ridge resident, was returning home from a friend's house late one Saturday night. This is her story:

"There are a lot of people who are going to say I'm nuts... I mean, I'll admit, I was tired that night. I had worked all day and then I watched a movie over at my boyfriend's house. I was ready for bed, for sure.

"I was passing the Grumman Park in Calverton when I noticed a couple of people walking towards Riverhead on the south side of Route 25. At first I thought they were fighting or dancing or something because they seemed to be moving around a lot, but when I looked closer I saw they were really just shadowy people and I could see right through them! They were people all right, but they weren't flesh and blood like us. They were ghosts! Some of them didn't have legs. Their bodies started at their torsos!

"I stepped on the gas so hard my car tore away from that spot like it was one of the jets Grumman put on display there. When I got home I woke up my mother and told her what I had seen. She sat with me in the dining room until early morning, telling me stories about family members who had seen ghosts. Apparently, it runs in the family."

Are the ghosts of former Grumman employees meeting nightly at the Grumman Memorial Park to remember better days from a bygone era or are they the ghosts of former military personnel strolling down the road from Calverton National Cemetery to admire the jets on display in the park?

Whether or not one of these scenarios is the case is impossible to say, but the next time you're driving by Grumman Memorial Park on Route 25 in Calverton you might want to whisper a thank you in memory of the thousands of men and woman whose hard work built Long Island and the jets that kept our country safe.

A sign reading "Calverton National Cemetery Ahead" stands at a lonely section of Route 25 in Calverton, a short distance west of Grumman Memorial Park.

The Talking Ghosts
of Yaphank's Woods

LOCATION: Eastbound service road of the
Long Island Expressway at Exit 67

DIRECTIONS: Take the Long Island Expressway east to Yaphank
Avenue (Exit 67) in Yaphank. At the end of the exit ramp is a traffic
light. Don't turn. Continue across Yaphank Avenue onto the service
road entrance at Exit 67 eastbound. Potter's Field Cemetery is located
on the right at the end of the service road.

Potter's Field Cemetery in Yaphank, now officially called "Almshouse Cemetery." This graveyard
is easily accessible to ghost enthusiasts who want to try their hand at ghost hunting.

Are There Mass Graves in the Woods?

For Long Island area ghost investigators, Almshouse Cemetery in Yaphank is a graveyard that just keeps giving!

Best known as Potter's Field Cemetery, many Long Island ghost hunters are already familiar with the graveyard's creepy black shadow people, suddenly appearing paranormal mists, and deathly-white apparitions stalking the night. But did you know that paranormal investigators also regularly hear the disembodied voices of the dead talking, humming, and even singing in the woods bordering the 140-year-old cemetery?

The woods around Potter's Field Cemetery where ghostly voices cry out in the night.

It's true. Investigators often hear voices from the woods that surround the cemetery, even more so than the voices coming from inside the cemetery itself!

During an autumn 2010 nighttime investigation, psychic-medium Joe Cahill of Lindenhurst was the first to take the issue of voices that people hear from the woods a step further.

Cahill said the disembodied voices investigators report hearing from the woods, particularly from the east and west sides of the graveyard, could be the voices of dead people calling out from mass graves. Investigators had reported hearing such voices on both sides of the cemetery during many investigations.

The haunted woods immediately outside Potter's Field Cemetery.

Already known widely by Long Island paranormal investigators for his stunning revelations at the Old Quaker Burying Ground cemeteries in Farmingdale, in which he was invaluable during the Long Island Devil Investigation in 2010, Cahill has now blazed a new trail at Potter's Field Cemetery for ghost investigators to pursue. He said he sensed different groups of people buried in the woods immediately outside the cemetery. He said he heard their spirits calling to him.

In an e-mail he sent The Paranormal Adventurers following an investigation he conducted with many Long Island ghost researchers, Cahill reported: "I felt a very Native American energy; and on the other side (east woods), I felt a very well... white energy... there is definitely a lot going on here. It was tough sorting through all the individuals."

If it's true that the spirits of dead people are stirring in these local woods and calling out for attention, then not only is the famously haunted Potter's Field Cemetery plagued by ghosts, but the woods around the cemetery are too! Since Cahill's initial report, other psychic-mediums have confirmed his readings.

Amanda Prag, from Lindenhurst, a ghost investigator on the nighttime investigation at Potter's Field, said: "I saw a black figure running through the woods right over there."

Prag, standing at the edge of the woods with a flashlight, pointed to a spot deep inside the trees where bright lights from the nearby county maintenance facility cast a milky background. "It looked like it was wearing a baseball cap... It just ran by!" she said.

A patch of white light is caught by a camera as it moved across the Suffolk County Farm and Education Center in Yaphank. Joseph Flammer, of The Paranormal Adventurers, watched it move from one side of the property to the other at the speed of a person running. "The anomaly was not caused by sunlight," said Flammer. "It gave off a glow of its own. I had been asking the spirits to show themselves and this one did." Flammer said the anomaly lasted about ten seconds and then wasn't seen again. The farm was where many of the residents of the Suffolk County Almshouse worked before they died and were buried in Potter's Field Cemetery.

Indeed, if the woods around the cemetery are haunted, then it is possible that the whole area, encompassing many dozens of acres and county-owned facilities on Yaphank Avenue, could be a huge portal to the other side.

Potter's Field Cemetery is a graveyard where more than 1,000 people were buried between 1872 and 1953. In 2010, the cemetery was officially named Almshouse Cemetery and a sign was erected by members of the Suffolk County Sheriff's Department over the entrance to the graveyard. Almost all the people buried in the graveyard were at one time residents of the Suffolk County Almshouse, also known as the Poorhouse, a place that took in poor, sick, and frail people who could not take care of themselves. The Almshouse was located on Yaphank Avenue.

"This is a crazy active area," Cahill summarized of the county property.

A nighttime investigation of Potter's Field Cemetery, conducted in mid-September 2010, was attended by twenty-five investigators. At this time, several psychic mediums said they sensed many spirits in the woods around the cemetery.

Cahill and another psychic he was working with, for example, said they sensed the spirits of between six and ten people buried together in one spot in the west woods, but that there were several more of these kinds of mass graves near the cemetery.

It's Cahill's belief that the bodies of people buried in one mass grave in the woods had been used in medical experiments. However, neither he nor the other mediums in attendance could determine whether or not the experiments were conducted by students, the military, or some kind of other organization. In the end, the psychics said they believed the experiments conducted on these people were probably performed in a hospital environment, possibly at the Almshouse.

While investigators consider the possibility of mass burials in the woods and search for answers as to how and why this could have happened, it should be kept in mind that these bodies could have been buried in the woods illegally. This kind of crime has plagued the bordering hamlet of Manorville for decades. On Halsey Manor Road, for example, dead bodies — some decapitated with their hands missing — have been discovered since the 1950s, local residents say. The kind of people who might have disposed of such bodies in the woods at Manorville could range from serial killers to gangsters.

Peggy Vetrano of Eastern Suffolk Paranormal addresses twenty-five investigators in a nighttime investigation at Potter's Field Cemetery on September 19, 2010. Vetrano, who led the investigation, is on a joint quest with William Sanchez, also of Eastern Suffolk Paranormal, to learn more about two people buried at Potter's Field whose names came through to them in EVPs in 2008.

Psychic-mediums pray with Joe Cahill (man in light shirt and glasses) in preparation for the September 19, 2010 nighttime investigation at Potter's Field Cemetery. Several mediums later that night said they psychically heard spirits calling out to them from the woods. Cahill believes that medical experiments had been conducted on some of the bodies buried in the woods.

In Potter's Field's case, the bodies could have been buried in the woods long before 1870 when the county purchased the land. In fact, the spot might have served local Native Americans as a burial ground long before the property became farmlands.

Cahill said he believes mass graves of black people and members of other non-white races are buried in the same woods as the bodies of persons on whom he believes experiments had been conducted. Old Suffolk County records indicate African Americans (called "colored" in the records) and Native Americans of the Shinnecock tribe (called "Pauper Indians" in the records) were buried side-by-side with white people in Potter's Field.

If these mass graves of African Americans and Native Americans do exist in the woods, the bodies might have been buried there long before the land was set aside by the county to serve as a cemetery. It might have been a family farm cemetery or an unofficial burial ground where poor people, such as local farmhands, were interred when they died. Such mass graves might have been a solution to quickly disposing of corpses of people who died of contagious diseases or groups of people who died in disasters. The mass burials might not have been malicious, sinister, or violent in nature, but practical.

"Anything could have happened here," noted one paranormal investigator, on edge as he searched the woods with his flashlight.

Paranormal investigator Mark Koenigsmann and his son Dave, of Massapequa Park, not only attended the September 19, 2010, investigation, but have also been a part of many other investigative sessions conducted at the site. They said that Cahill's psychic discovery of mass graves in the scraggy bushes and tall brown and green pine trees of county-owned woods makes a lot of sense to them since they have, on several occasions, heard the voices of the dead coming from the shadowy woods.

"It makes sense that the psychics are saying voices are coming from the woods," said Mark, a former EMT. "The dead want us to know they are here. When you hear their voices, they almost always sound like they are coming from the woods, not the graveyard!"

The Koenigsmanns said they had always found this unexpected paranormal occurrence of voices from the woods confusing because they were detecting more spiritual activity amongst the trees of the woods than in the hallowed graveyard itself. However, one night, Mark Koenigsmann said, he saw a girl dressed in colonial period clothing walking across the graveyard, only to disappear, indicating there is also plenty of paranormal activity connected to the cemetery, too.

Loads of Questions to be Answered

How could it be that bodies were buried in mass unmarked graves at this place? After all, this property has been owned and watched over by Suffolk County since 1870. We have to ask:

1) Were there dead buried in the woods before the cemetery was a cemetery?

2) Were bodies dumped illegally in the woods without the county's knowledge?

3) Did markers on the mass graves get destroyed, stolen, or rot away?

4) What happened to these people that they had to be buried in mass graves? Did they have a communicable disease? Were they killed by gangsters or serial killers and buried in the middle of the night? Or were some people who lived in the Poorhouse buried in heaps to save the time and effort of performing individual burials?

Mounds in the woods beside Potter's Field Cemetery. Are these the result of dirt that was dumped in piles in the woods, or could there be bodies under these mounds? According to psychics, there are bodies buried somewhere in these woods.

While nobody may ever know precisely what happened to the people who are now ghosts in the woods — if there really are any bodies buried in the woods — psychic Janet Russell of Medford, like many others psychics who investigated the place, believes there's more to Potter's Field than meets the eye.

Russell, a psychic-medium and host of *Beyond the Unexplained*, a Cablevision public access television show, said she, too, believes there are unmarked graves in the area. Specifically, Russell said during an interview taped for her television show in May 2010, that she sensed members of a large family were buried together at Potter's Field. County records do not list such a family buried in the cemetery.

"They're here because they died in a terrible fire and they had no other place to go," the medium said into the lens of the video camera trained on her for her television show as she explored the graves of Potter's Field at night.

It was Russell's spearheading efforts in 2010 that was largely responsible for inspiring members of the Suffolk County Sheriff's Department to contribute private donations to upgrade Potter's Field Cemetery with handsome wooden split rail fences around two areas of graves. The fences, erected shortly after Russell visited the cemetery for the first time with Diane and I, were intended to be a symbolic gesture of remembrance for the poor souls buried there.

In addition, the cemetery, which had for so long been referred to simply as "Potter's Field," was given the formal name "Almshouse Cemetery" to reflect its connection to the Suffolk County Almshouse, previously also known as the Poorhouse, also known as the Suffolk County Insane Asylum, also known by a few other disturbing names.

A formal memorial for the souls of Almshouse Cemetery was held on the morning of Memorial Day 2010 and attended by Russell, clergy, a singing group, and members of the Suffolk County Sheriff's Department.

The graves of the men, women, and children who were buried in the cemetery between 1872 and 1953 are marked by simple small stones that bare only numbers, not the names of the people buried in the graves. This may have had much to do with disapproving social attitudes towards poor, mentally ill, and developmentally disabled persons during the years the Almshouse was in operation.

Thus, even in death, the residents of the Poorhouse were once again punished by society for being substandard citizens because of their inability to provide for themselves. Rather than being seen as people who needed help dealing with personal problems beyond their control, the residents of the Almshouse were negatively perceived as living off the charity of the county's taxpayers.

The grave markers at Potter's Field Cemetery indicate the residents were treated more like numbers than people. Apparently, once dead, they were not worthy to be buried with stones that listed their names. One can just envision the officials of the Almshouse yelling at a meeting, "Stones with names are just too damn expensive! They're lucky to have anything! Good riddance to them all!"

Spirits Calling Out for Attention

Russell's psychic vision of a family whose members died in a fire could not be confirmed with the county's burial records from Almshouse Cemetery. This was a vision that came to her while she was being interviewed at the edge of the cemetery's woods, where Cahill, Mark Koenigsmann, Diane, and I, as well as many other investigators, have heard disembodied voices.

Russell sensed the spirits of these five family members as she was walking towards the graves from the road on a spring night in 2010. Diane and I were interviewing her for a segment we did on her television show. The hour-long program featured The Paranormal Adventurers and psychic John Altieri, who had been physically touched on the back by a spirit in the cemetery on the night we shot the interview. There's video of this event on our website: www.paranormaladventurers.com.

The phenomenon of investigators feeling taps on their bodies is common in Potter's Field. Whether these taps are delivered to people by spirits from the graveyard or spirits from the woods is impossible to say.

Denise Reilly, of West Babylon, who had been one of the lead investigators of the Long Island Devil Investigation in Farmingdale, experienced tapping on her shoulder while standing in front a large group of investigators gathered in Potter's Field Cemetery on the night of the September 19, 2010 investigation.

"I was just touched on my shoulder!" Reilly announced in a sharp voice, interrupting an EVP session. Her eyes darted to shadows as she quickly scanned the area for any signs of ghosts. "Just now... I was tapped!"

The most active spots in the cemetery for disembodied voices and photos of strange anomalies are the northwest corner near the woods and diagonally across the graveyard, at the southeast corner, also near the woods.

It was on the east side of the cemetery, near the south corner of the graveyard, where Lisa Barrow, an author from Speonk, said she heard voices in the night. Lisa, who wrote *Love in the Gardens of Macantar: A Spiritual Journey of Healing from Codependency and Relationship Addiction*, under the name Lisa Acor Laurel, listened intently to the sounds of the night as she and other intrigued investigators conducted an EVP session to try to capture spirit responses to questions they posed. "How did you die?" one of the investigators asked as they huddled in a circle under the moon. "Were you murdered?"

While Lisa's book, *Love in the Gardens of Macantar*, is largely about relationships between people, on this night, as a paranormal enthusiast, Lisa was focusing on the relationship between the spirits of deceased humans and the living. She kept a watchful eye out for moving ghosts at the dark tree line at the edge of the woods.

John Dickson, an investigator from Levittown, suddenly heard "a party" of voices wash out of the woods closer to the north end of the eastern side of the cemetery at the same time as Lisa and other researchers were conducting the EVP session. He was only a hundred feet away from Lisa and her group, but they didn't hear what he heard. Dickson was not alone, though. Several other people standing beside him also heard voices wafting from the woods at that second. They searched the towering army of marching trees with the stark beams of their powerful flashlights, revealing nothing.

Diane and I were with Dickson's group and we heard the utterances, as well.

Meanwhile, the voices of the investigators in Lisa group suddenly swelled melodically from across the moonscape graveyard, bathed now in a blue lunar haze as midnight approached evermore steadfastly, for they, too, suddenly heard voices calling out for attention from the woods. Excitedly, they, too, craned their necks and searched eagerly with crisscrossing beams of flashlights for the source, but there was nothing there to see.

Investigations Continue

While loud noises continually rush into the graveyard from the nearby Long Island Expressway, the ghostly voices heard by investigators sound human enough, yet strangely, they also sound as if they are spoken from an underground location or from behind an invisible shield that somehow diminishes their strength. If it wasn't for this diminishment, the voices probably would sound as if spoken in regular human conversational tones — for they are not typically whispered, but spoken at the normal level. These utterances, which regularly possess this mysterious distant quality, cannot be readily explained nor can their distant quality. Some people might suggest the voices have to pass through a spiritual veil in order to reach people's ears. Investigators continue to probe the woods and cemetery to find out more. *(Through our many investigations, Diane and I have found the best time to hear and see the spirits of Almshouse Cemetery is during the witching hour — between 2 and 3 o'clock in the morning.)*

An orb looms over Diane Hill while she studies an area of soft, freshly dug-up dirt near the woods. What was buried here recently and why? While this orb has all the concentric tell-tale signs of being just a typical dust orb, it is nonetheless an eerie reminder of nights when orbs appeared to investigators' naked eyes and people were physically touched or heard voices.

While not all voices heard by investigators in the cemetery are from the woods — some are clearly spoken by spirits from areas inside the cemetery itself — it might behoove curious investigators to conduct EVP sessions to try to ascertain information that could be employed as "triggers," said Peggy Vetrano, of Southampton, who led a series of well-attended nighttime investigations at the cemetery in 2010, including the famous September 19th and October 31st investigations so often referred to in this writing. These triggers can be useful in asking the spirits pertinent questions and enhancing the possibility of making more revealing contacts, she said.

Vetrano and William Sanchez, members of the Long Island paranormal research group Eastern Suffolk Paranormal, are on a mission — they are relentlessly continuing their investigation of two specific names they received while conducting EVP sessions at Potter's Field in 2008. In separate EVPs, Vetrano and Sanchez recorded the names

The Problem with Stone 1023

Could there be mass graves in the woods? While investigators try to solve this mystery through efforts to contact the dead and engage them in a dialog, Diane and I are also pursuing other questions to which we are hoping to find concrete answers.

One such question centers on a grave marker we, along with Mark and David Koenigsmann, discovered broken and lying abandoned at the edge of the woods. While it is exactly like the others stones in the cemetery, the stone we found stood out because it is marked with the number "1023" on in its surface. The problem with this stone is that records show there never was a grave 1023 in the cemetery.

According to country records, there are only 1,013 graves in the Potter's Field Cemetery. The obvious question arises: If there is a marker for 1023, where are the ten bodies that are not accounted for in the graveyard's records? Are they in the woods?

According to the county's records, only 1,013 people are buried in Potter's Field Cemetery. Why did we discover a stone for grave 1023 at the edge of the woods — and where did this marker go (see *opposite page*)? *Photo of stone by Mark Koenigsmann.*

Even if the county purchased grave markers in quantities so large that it never used most of, let's say, the last fifty markers, why was the marker on the edge of the graveyard and not in a warehouse with numbers 1021, 1022, 1024, etc. — if such stones even exist? Why was only 1023 found?

Marker 1023 has since been stolen, discarded by groundskeepers, or moved to a location where we can no longer find it. We're hoping it was moved and not stolen because we are familiar with terrible stories of doom for those who steal gravestones from cemeteries. We have heard stories of grave thieves coming to horrific, tragic ends.

Maybe some of the voices people hear from the woods are those belonging to ghosts of graves from which markers have disappeared over time. Maybe the spirits are calling out from the woods to be remembered the way those buried in the cemetery have been remembered, with memorials, visits by the public, and acknowledgments that they once existed and are worth remembering, too.

Stone marker 1023 was taken from this spot. *(See opposite page)*

Section Two:
Ghouls and Monsters

The Halloween Night Ghoul of Potter's Field

LOCATION: Eastbound service road of the
Long Island Expressway at Exit 67

DIRECTIONS: Take the Long Island Expressway east to Yaphank Avenue (Exit 67) in Yaphank. At the end of the exit ramp is a traffic light. Don't turn. Continue across Yaphank Avenue onto the service road entrance at Exit 67 eastbound. Potter's Field Cemetery is located on the right at the end of the service road.

The end of the Long Island Expressway service road going eastbound at Exit 67 in Yaphank. Potter's Field Cemetery is located on the other side of the guard rail at the extreme right of the photo. To visit the cemetery, drivers can park their vehicles along the curb and merely step over the guardrail. The graves start immediately.

They Only Come Out At Night

Our blood-curdling, incredible story of fate and the wandering gray ghoul of Potter's Field Cemetery in Yaphank begins with Diane turning her SUV easterly at the green traffic light on Yaphank Avenue. The vehicle's bright headlights pierced the dark night as we took the left turn, drawing us into a well-known haunted forest.

In front of us appeared the dense woods that are referred to as the Pine Barrens. This ancient forest of pitch pine and scrub oak trees is preserved and protected by the government because the roots of the trees filter rainwater into drinking water.

Yaphank has enormous tracts of pine barrens. In fact, this forest where our story begins stretches many miles to the south, into Southaven Park in the hamlet of Brookhaven. Some people claim Southaven Park is the site where a UFO crashed many years ago. Allegedly, dead extraterrestrials were taken from the ship by men in black uniforms. None of the black

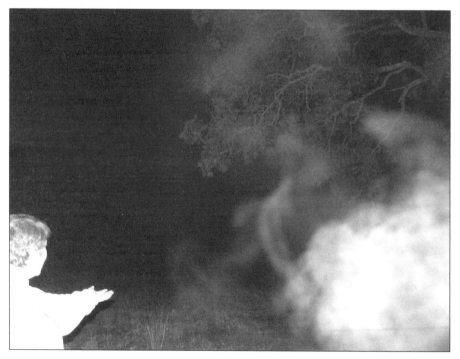

Diane Hill makes contact with a ghost at Potter's Field Cemetery in Yaphank. The ghost spoke to Diane and Joseph Flammer and held Diane's hand. This occurred at 2:30 in the morning, during the witching hour.

uniforms bore insignias of the secretive government agencies the men represented, witnesses claimed at the time. Some people alleged that the bodies of the dead extraterrestrials were brought to Brookhaven National Lab in Upton for autopsies. Of course, authorities at the Lab have denied all of this.

As we took that fateful left turn onto the Long Island Expressway's desolate service road, we had no idea that we were about to come face-to-face with one of the most perplexing mysteries we had ever encountered as investigators and reporters of the paranormal. For in the bright beams of the headlights we suddenly caught our first sight of the gray man who would haunt our imaginations and dreams for months to come.

Diane and I, and a few other people who saw him, have mixed feelings about the nature of this person, with Diane and I suspecting the man may not have been human. Rather, we have reason to believe he was actually a ghoul from Potter's Field Cemetery.

Do you see the outline of the tall figure with a shirt sleeve rolled up his arm standing in front of Diane? The ghost took hold of Diane's hand and held it. This is one of the many ghosts of Potter's Field Cemetery.

Dead Man Walking

Oddly, the first thing I noticed most immediately about this man was not his strange, slow, painful gait or his unworldly gray demeanor. It was not even the peculiar way he was holding his gut at his left side, as if he had been stabbed or shot in the abdomen. No, the first thing I noticed about him was the strands of his dark hair falling violently into his eyes and bouncing against his pale, waxen forehead as he walked in a slow shuffle, an obviously labored and painful sort of gallop, the awkward strides of which did not advance him much, but did make the act of walking, in this case, appear to be a wrenched task.

He did not have long hair. In fact, the hair at the sides of his head was shaved, but the hair at the front of his head was longer. Perhaps when he was alive this man combed back these bouncing front strands neatly onto the top of his head. Maybe, because of his current circumstance, being dead and all, it no longer mattered to him if his hair was not neat. Maybe, it no longer mattered to him that he even had hair. Maybe nothing of this world mattered to him any longer.

Neither Diane nor I could see this enigma's eyes. The thick cover of darkness seemed to shoot a sharp black blade of impenetrable unknowing across his eyes, but I suspect his eyes were gray, too, just like his skin.

As far as we could tell the man didn't even acknowledge us with so much as a curious glance as we pulled slowly alongside him in his awkward, tilted, shuffling sort of march into the mystery of the waning crescent-moon October night, seemingly from out of nowhere, seemingly going nowhere.

The wide margin of grass in front of the woods as seen from in front of the cemetery and looking towards Yaphank Avenue (around a bend in the far distance). The ghoul of Potter's Field walked from Yaphank Avenue to the cemetery.

The only thing we could tell for sure was that he was headed the way we were headed...to the bleak cemetery at the end of the dark, lonely road. It's a haunted place where the dead seem to wake up in the night. Was the cemetery the ghoul's home? His nightly origin? His nocturnal ending? Did he exist only at twilight, like a vampire, and mindlessly pace the soulless dark?

Halloween Night Ghost Hunt

Understand, this was not any ordinary Long Island night and this was not an ordinary Long Island place. It was the chilled autumn night of the big ghost hunt in Potter's Field Cemetery. Ghost investigators from all across Long Island were congregating at the end of the service road at this very instant. Diane and I were half an hour late. The people who had already gathered were waiting for us and other late-comers to arrive before starting the event. We knew the ghost hunters would be anxious to get started because it was Halloween night, a time out of time. Halloween is believed to be a night when the veil between our world and the world beyond is at its thinnest. Anything could happen.

Potter's Field Cemetery is a place wherein a thousand souls are buried, the last put in the ground in 1953. Those of us attending the ghost hunt this evening were searching for ghosts or at least evidence of them. Potter's Field is an established haunted location. Contact with the spirit world has been made here in the past. Many of us tonight wanted to build upon past experiences with the spirits in residence and, in fact, on this very night a woman would see a black figure darting through the woods near the cemetery and others would see orbs floating over graves with their naked eyes.

Communication would be made with spirits using electronic devices such as a K-2 Meter, an Ovilus, and voice recorders that yielded the voices of disembodied spirits in the form of EVPs. With our own ears, we would, hopefully, hear spirits talking, laughing, and crying in the primordial woods that border the graveyard on three sides.

At one time this whole area of Yaphank was composed of farmland and forest. In 1870, Suffolk County bought 170 acres of this land from a farmer and set up county facilities on it. To this day, Suffolk County maintains a complex of office buildings and farmlands on Yaphank Avenue.

One of the county facilities that has gone by the wayside over the years is the Poorhouse, otherwise known as the Almshouse. It was a place where sick, frail, and poor people lived. These were people who could not financially provide for themselves. There is much evidence to suggest that people who lived in the Poorhouse were treated badly by the staff.

When these same people died, they were carted across Yaphank Avenue from the Poorhouse, then five minutes away by horse-drawn hearse, to this timid, quiet cemetery where tonight we would be ghost hunting. At night, the ghosts of this cemetery are screaming to be heard, perhaps because as people they were neglected in life.

This isolated location, this dark, foreboding place of ghosts, is unlike any other graveyard Diane and I have ever investigated in Suffolk County. The cemetery is situated at the end of the eastbound service road where it enters onto the Long Island Expressway at Exit 67. This is a no man's land. There are no houses around, no stores to shop — only woods, graves, the road, and indifference.

The sounds of diesel trucks with gears winding sorrowfully down as they barrel along at seventy miles an hour, the rubber of their tires crying forlornly on the hard, black pavement, while cars and smaller trucks whiz along the regretful highway, roaring uncaringly onward in a gloom akin to remorse that is so well known by people who have broken down or hitch-hiked on cold roads late at night; all the sad sounds wafting up and altogether in a whirlwind of gritty night air, a symphony of gloom sung to the service road and shouted into the stark grandstand of the graveyard wherein eyes of the dead follow us.

The ghoul was a thin man, narrow at the shoulders and hips. His face appeared gaunt, haggard. He did not appear to be young. He was between thirty and forty years of age, but because he looked dead... Well, it was hard to tell.

There was a tiredness about him, a weariness that bespoke turmoil and personal loss. Maybe he was telling us his story as we watched him weave the incomprehensible tapestry of his death and doom with his feet on the cold grass as he walked, leaving a tale for us to consider in his post-mortem wake, as, indeed, we are doing right now. If so, we still cannot glimpse what his sad story was ,or how his life played-out like water going down a drain, and we'll probably never know any of the details. Maybe he'll get to tell somebody else who happens by these woods some night. Maybe that person will understand what we did not.

Like the dead man in the 1993 movie *Weekend at Bernie's II*, the ghoul seemed to be propelled along the edge of the forest in the direction of the cemetery by a force greater than himself, by visceral Death itself: a dead man merely making the strutting motions across the stage, but not actually participating in his morbid encore on Earth. How or why this would happen was, and still is, well beyond our understanding, but there he was walking in front of us — gray and as dead as a dead man can look.

The strange apparition appeared to be wearing a gray, light, military-styled jacket, the design of which was unfamiliar to both Diane and I; however, I would venture to guess that it was a Civil War garment. His baggy dark pants seemed to be held up by a wide black leather Garrison belt and his boots appeared to be black and buckled like a hunter who chases leprechauns. Above all, it was obvious to us that he was clearly inappropriately dressed for the cold autumn weather through which he painfully plowed onward.

At the time we did not think he was a ghoul, so we considered momentarily the reason why this odd, sickly man was out and about in the Pine Barrens — the coldest part of Long Island — in late October, alone and without even a flashlight to aid him in his slow trek on the rugged terrain. Remember, with the waning crescent moon, not even forty percent of the moon's light was available to aid him in seeing the terrain clearly. If he was a man, he was taking his chances. If he was a ghoul, well... he was out of chances.

Surely, as the temperatures plummeted throughout the frosty night, this out-of-sorts fellow was bound to become hypothermic. There was also a good chance he would injure an ankle or break a knee in a sudden dip or hole in the uneven grass where he walked.

Where could he have been walking to? This was the greatest mystery, though there were three possible answers to this all-important question: the cemetery, the woods, or the long, black, unforgiving highway that snaked out before him with no comforts to offer. After all, there was no other place to go in the direction he was walking. If pressed by a judge in court, I'd have to say he was walking back to his grave, but that's only because I actually saw him and sensed the tragedy that walked with him. I don't expect others who didn't see him to comprehend his ghastly unearthliness.

The ghoul carried nothing as he mindlessly meandered, slowly, a wide margin of grass alongside the woods that run all the way from Yaphank Avenue to the end of the service road and the graveyard. The grass path that he walked is like a wide margin on the side of the long green page of woods — and this margin is twenty feet wide.

At the end of the service road, the margin blends into the open space of the grassy cemetery. From there, it mingles into nights of secrecy, of lives lost, and deaths not yet accepted by the dead. It was the dead of Potter's Field that we were here tonight to glean, if only the spirits would allow.

The ghoul stared straight ahead into the unknowing abyss of darkness that lay before him. What was most striking about this alleged man was that he appeared to be favoring his left side, tilting into his left rib cage, holding his left gut, as if he had been injured in the belly.

The strands of dark hair bouncing into his eyes, his hands holding his side as if he was preventing his guts from spilling out, all of it smacking of a man who had received a gunshot and was now staggering homeward for the last time to say goodbye to his wife and kids. He would never reach them.

We took a good look at this man as we passed. We wondered if we knew him. Perhaps he was joining us on the ghost hunt tonight. Though still far off, it was apparent he was walking in the direction of the group of investigators congregated in the darkness outside the cemetery. We had spotted these people in the hollow orbs of Diane's headlights far down the road.

Diane and I looked at each other after we passed the man.

"Who's he?" Diane asked.

"I don't know," I answered.

"He doesn't look right," Diane said.

"I agree. He's scary looking."

Diane steered her gray and black SUV, a box shaped Honda Element, down the road, leaving the ghoul way behind as I watched him disappear in the passenger-side mirror.

In the headlights, we saw up ahead were many cars, about ten or eleven, parked one behind the other along the curb at the edge of the wide grass margin. The cars stretched in a long line to the graveyard. There, spread out in the midst of the woods like a huge picnic blanket, lay the maintained lawn and the thousand graves. We knew these cars belonged to ghost investigators. It seemed that nobody but deer hunters and ghost investigators ever parked here, and tonight there would be no hunters around.

We pulled over at the end of the long line of cars, to be the twelfth vehicle. Diane turned off the lights. Meanwhile, a car entered the service road from Yaphank Avenue and illuminated the ghostly-looking bodies of people waiting outside the cemetery to start the hunt. The car flew passed us and shot off to the left, onto the LIE. The car then joined the other vehicles with moving headlights shooting swiftly along the east and westbound sides of the road down in the lower canyon of open space, beyond the bushes, that was the tumultuous Long Island Expressway of rural eastern Long Island.

I looked into the side mirror. "Don't get out yet," I said to Diane. "That guy we saw back there is coming this way and he worries me. Let's just wait till he passes. Let's take a good look at him."

"Okay," said Diane, and she tilted the rear-view mirror to get a better look at him as he approached the SUV from behind. "Where is he?" she asked.

"He's still way back there. Lock the doors and keep all the interior lights off. We'll just wait here a few minutes for him to pass."

I had a cell phone in my hand, ready to call the police if this man should prove to be a lunatic or in any way cause us or anybody else trouble. What reason did he have to be in this area on the very night we were holding a ghost hunt? Was this stranger up to something unfriendly? Could he be a ghost hunter whom Diane and I had not yet met? Was he walking down to the group to join in the hunt? It seemed unlikely to us.

The dark of the forbidden night seeped into the box vehicle, hiding us away from the ghoul, as we sat silently waiting for him. In a few minutes he appeared closer in the mirrors. Before long he was walking beside the Element in a lifeless walk, a slow gallop, holding his left side, like a soldier from the Civil War who had been shot by a sniper and was now dying. He did not look anywhere but straight ahead towards the cemetery.

We had earlier prepared our psyches for the ghost hunt that lay ahead of us, but not for this. Not for an actual brush-up with an entity imitating a man.

Why hadn't this supposed man even glanced at our car? Certainly, he saw us pull over to the curb, and surely, he must have seen that we didn't get out of the vehicle yet. Or is it just me who thinks that this man acted negligently for not taking an active interest in his own safety? After all, Diane and I could have been thieves waiting to jump him for his money or serial killers looking for a new victim. He didn't know who we were or why we sat, waiting, in a dark car in a lonely place under the cover of night. His life could have been in jeopardy — that is, if he were alive to begin with.

Had We Met This Ghoul Before?

Could this ghoul be the very man Diane and I saw walk out into traffic without regard for oncoming cars on another night we were driving through the historic hamlet of Yaphank, weeks earlier?

I am reluctant to even share this story, for the mere memory of it still makes me quake, but I can't help but wonder if the ghoul had introduced himself to us another time. Could our prior experience with him be a bizarre connection to Potter's Field?

It was an oppressively dark evening and the black sky was laden with an oncoming storm that would soon rage from out of the south, but hadn't yet hit. Only a few big drops of rain had splashed on our vehicle's windshield as a prelude to what was about to explode over Long Island.

We were making our way south towards the Long Island Expressway to go to another part of Long Island to investigate a haunted house wherein the woman who owned the house said shameful things happened in her bedroom at night. She said a black being appeared to her at night and would touch her. Her husband, who lies next to her in bed at night, has witnessed the grotesque entity and its foul debauchery, and she wanted the entity out of her life.

Diane and I were talking about this most frightening of cases and what we could do to force the entity to appear to us so we could document it, when, just as we approached the famous Mill House Inn in Yaphank, a man walked out before our vehicle.

The Mill House Inn is a well known and respected restaurant and bar with a long-standing solid reputation for being a good place to eat, drink, and listen to live music. It's located at the fringe of picturesque Mill Pond.

Our friend Janet Russell, a well-known Long Island psychic-medium from Medford, often does psychic readings of people at the Mill House Inn. She told us the place is haunted. According to Janet, things move on their own and the staff sees ghostly things that shouldn't be. She also told us that management was agreeable to a ghost investigation. Janet invited us to participate in an investigation, but because of our conflicting schedules, we were never able to join her in a search for ghosts at the Mill House Inn.

The Mill House Inn. It was from the edge of the parking lot where a man stepped out into heavy traffic at night without caring about his safety. Was the man actually the Ghoul of Potter's Field Cemetery that people saw on Halloween night?

It was at the instant we were approaching the Inn that a man suddenly appeared out of nowhere from the edge of the parking lot and up to the road — all in a flash — and stepped off the curb. We don't know if he was actually coming from the parking lot of he restaurant or materialized into our world at that exact moment. Regardless, traffic was thick as fleas at that hour because it was a Sunday evening and Sundays always inspire heavy traffic in eastern Long Island. People from Manhattan and Queens who had spent the weekend out east now have to return home. Drivers were pressing on each other to hurry up to get to the expressway, a mile south on narrow County Road 21, the very road that we were on at the moment passing through pretty Yaphank hamlet. Diane was driving close to the car in front of us, and the car behind us was practically tailgating.

The man we saw appeared gray and walked stiffly at a zombie-like pace. We saw him suddenly appear from out of nowhere and step out of the edge of the parking lot and right into the street in front of us without looking. He didn't seem to notice or care that cars were aimed right at him, that our vehicle and other 4,000-pound vehicles were moving at thirty miles an hour or better, right for his body.

Diane slammed on her brakes and sent the Element skidding on the loose gravel. The car came to a screeching halt within inches of the ghoulish figure. We were badly shaken up, but the man just continued his zombie-like walk without acknowledging the fact he was almost killed, as he simply crossed into the oncoming traffic on the northbound side of the narrow road. Vehicles on that side of the street also suddenly screeched on the pavement as drivers tried to avoid hitting him.

We agreed that neither of us had ever seen a human so obviously oblivious to danger as this man — that is, if he was a man. He never even flinched as Diane's SUV flew towards him. We didn't believe he was drunk because he was not staggering. His pace was slow and deliberate. Our gut feeling was that he was not coming from the restaurant, but rather he came from out of thin air.

I looked back to see if the man had gotten hit by a vehicle on the other side of the road, but he was nowhere to be seen. Cars had pulled over in the loud confusion. No doubt the drivers were also searching to see where the man had gone. We pulled off to the side as well and wondered if we had just seen a ghost. The idea that it was a ghoul was far from our thinking at that time. It wasn't until we saw the ghoul of Potter's Field Cemetery that we thought in retrospect to that night we almost ran over a man in front of the haunted Inn.

Finally, not seeing a corpse on the pavement, the drivers who had stopped on the road took off. Diane stepped on the gas and we got out of there too. We were truly shook up for the rest of the night because we came within inches of killing a human being, we thought, and it wouldn't have been Diane's fault.

We don't know who that man was or why it was that he so obviously wanted to die. Surely, either the man was trying to commit suicide or he was so mentally unstable that not even his sense of self-preservation kicked in as our vehicle screeched before him. He didn't even blink in the headlights or look at us as we just missed running him over. It was an event that was far from normal — and it happened in Yaphank, roughly a mile from Potter's Field Cemetery, where we were now, watching the ghoul approaching us as we sat in Diane's Element in the dark of night.

The Ghoul Enters Potter's Field

We had been to Potter's Field Cemetery more times than we could remember; and, like many other investigators, we had first-hand knowledge of the place being abundantly haunted. Here we have *seen*, *heard*, and *felt* things during the night and also during the day. However, to the best of our knowledge, neither Diane nor I have ever seen a life-like, full-bodied apparition, or a ghoul, anywhere, ever! This would be a first for both of us. We have seen ghosts, the white misty type, and the hollow-looking human type, and the black shadow people type, but never ones that perfectly resembled three-dimensional, solid human beings right down to the boots.

We had the distinct feeling we might be seeing a full-bodied apparition or a ghoul tonight, but it wouldn't be till later, when we had a report that other people saw him — when it was impossible that they could have — that we started to wonder if we had witnessed a supernatural phenomenon.

We watched the gray, skinny man walk through the dark towards the cemetery alongside the long line of cars belonging to fellow ghost investigators. In the light of headlights belonging to a car that turned onto the service road and was building up speed to enter onto the LIE, we watched the ghoul approach the large group of investigators who were standing together with much gesticulating and motion. The ghoul simply bypassed the group and veered off to the right. He came within a few yards of the group before he climbed the low guardrail that separates the road from the cemetery and disappeared into the black oblivion of the tortured night...alone and without the aid of a flashlight or a warm jacket.

Diane and I had not expected him to bypass the group. At the time, we thought he was a very different kind of man, and yes, strange, but since to the best of our knowledge we had never seen a ghoul before, we fully expected that he was a real flesh and blood human being, maybe even someone who was joining us and the other investigators on the ghost hunt on this night. We shook our heads, grabbed our equipment, and talked for a moment outside Diane's SUV about what we had just seen.

Just then, our two good friends, sisters-in-laws Denise Reilly of West Babylon and Denise Reilly of Little Neck, rolled up in a car behind us. We had seen their car's headlights approaching from far away at Yaphank Avenue and saw that the car was pulling over slowly to the curb to line up with the other cars in the long line aimed down to the blackened burial ground. Theirs would be vehicle number thirteen. I know this because I counted the cars.

We immediately expressed our concern about this man to Denise and Denise, telling them we thought he might be dangerous, and that now he was in the cemetery or in the nearby woods where we were all going. We told them we had to alert people, that he could be dangerous.

Denise Reilly and Denise Reilly, sisters-in-law, were lead investigators during the Long Island Devil Investigation of 2010. Denise (on right) saw the ghoul of Potter's Field at the same place where Joseph Flammer and Diane Hill saw him only a moment earlier, when it could not have been possible.

A look of consternation fell over one of the woman's faces, as she said, "We just saw him... It sounds like the same guy. We saw him walking this way from Yaphank Avenue — just now as we pulled up."

"You couldn't have," I exclaimed. "He just entered the cemetery. It would take him at least ten minutes at the speed he was walking to return back to the spot where you say you saw him, and even if he could get there in time, we didn't see him pass back this way, so it couldn't have been him."

The four of us stood next to the cars and went over every aspect of this event that we and they had witnessed. Was the man actually a ghost replaying his walk for us and other people who happened upon this spot on this Halloween night?

"In order for him to return where you saw him, he'd have to run at full speed through the woods without a flashlight in the dark of night, and it's doubtful that even if he ran as fast as an Olympian, he could cover even half the distance back to Yaphank Avenue, and much more likely that he'd slam his head right into a tree in the darkness and knock himself out!" I insisted. "Why on earth would he run back to the spot where you saw him and where we saw him a few minutes earlier...so he could re-walk the walk he just walked?" I asked.

"We agree," said the women, only one of which had actually seen the man as they drove down the service road. "It doesn't make sense." They held firm to the story about the same man, dressed the same way, holding his same side. It was definitely the same apparition.

Eventually, the four of us walked down to the cemetery and joined the other ghost investigators who were milling about in the dark in front of the graveyard. After saying our hellos to everyone, we inquired about the man. We described him and asked if anybody knew him, but it appeared that none of them did. He had not accompanied any of them to the hunt.

We followed up, asking if anyone had seen him enter the cemetery.

One investigator, Gabe Falsetta of Bethpage, a member of the Long Island Paranormal Detectives (LIPD), said his ghost hunting friend and LIPD member, Jim Kenny of North Bellmore, did see a man in the area.

A chill came over us.

Jim Kenny said he thought he saw the same man we saw. He remembered the man walking by him and Gabe while they were standing beside their vehicle, which was parked directly in front of Diane's SUV.

In a conversation about the man months later, Jim remembered the man's strange look as he passed him and Gabe, and he remembered commenting to me about this disheveled man when he and Gabe joined Diane, Denise Reilly, Denise Reilly, and I as we walked from the cars to the ghost hunting group, though I have no recollection of this, probably because I was fumbling with cameras by then, and exchanging welcomes with a flood of people as we approached.

In an e-mail written days after seeing the man, and in response to an inquiry, Jim said he did see a "thin, sickly" man in the area before the ghost investigation got underway, and he thought he saw the man smoking a cigarette. He, too, thought the man looked strange, perhaps

The Angry Ghosts of Sweet Hollow Road

LOCATION: The woods of West Hills Nature Preserve, on Mount Misery between Old Country Road and the Northern State Parkway

DIRECTIONS: Take the Long Island Expressway to Exit 49 North (Route 110, also known locally as Broad Hollow Road). Go approximately a half-mile and make a left on Sweet Hollow Road. If you get lost, go to the Sweet Hollow Diner on the west side of Route 110. Sweet Hollow Road is located only a hundred feet south of the diner.

A nighttime paranormal mist covers the entrance to West Hills Nature Preserve on Sweet Hollow Road. Photographing such mists on Sweet Hollow Road and inside the woods of the nature preserve at night is not uncommon, even in the heart of summer. These mists are not "fogs." Rather, they are believed by many ghost investigators to be manifestations of spirits.

Hitting, Yelling Spirits

Nowhere on Long Island are ghosts more accessible or terrifying than on lonely Sweet Hollow Road in Melville.

The darkness of this mysterious country road, located off busy Route 110, a corridor of commerce in central Long Island, is so profound that none but the most hardy and knowledgeable of ghost hunters dares visit the woods here at night to commune with ghosts. Wannabe investigators and thrill seekers tend to just walk into the woods for a quick peek or never get out of their cars while visiting at night. Instead of seeking out the real places where ghosts reside, they trespass a local graveyard as a poor substitute for actually being in the deep of the woods with the angry spirits that plague the area, but, really, who can blame them? It's dangerous in the woods at night. Stay away!

The Snake Pit

There are many scary incidents reported by people who have experienced the road's... well, let's say... sinister personality.

Ghostly visitations range from white horses appearing in snowstorms in the wee hours of the morning — leaving no tracks in the high snow drifts before vanishing into the oblivion of the haunted woods — to the ghosts of long-dead soldiers and forlorn women from another time period.

Shades of deceased persons appear on the sides of the road as translucent white figures or sometimes black shadows.

A face captured on a log in the woods of Sweet Hollow Road. This strange phenomenon is familiar to ghost investigators who visit Sweet Hollow Road. Are the spirits creating these faces, or is it just coincidence that faces appear naturally in the bark of trees and on logs?

If you're planning on entering the woods along Sweet Hollow Road, the nature preserve entrance is probably the best spot to do it. However, the problem with this spot is that there are only enough parking spaces in front of the nature preserve entrance for about five cars and that's only if you use both sides of the road. These parking spaces are just dirt spots that have been created by tires over the years from people who wanted to park their vehicles directly in front of the preserve's entrance. Except for these two small spots, there are no shoulders at the sides of Sweet Hollow Road.

As a result, if you have a group of more than four cars, as paranormal clubs often do, you will find parking difficult, which is why a lot of people choose to park on Gwynne Road, located on the north side of the overpass, and then walk south to the preserve entrance. Walking on the road, of course, is risky because there is not much room to avoid cars coming up from behind.

In daylight, people who need to park might drive their vehicles down to Sweet Hollow Hall (a county-owned facility at the end of the gated road that goes into the woods where Sweet Hollow Road intersects with Gwynne Road), where people can park during the day and hike Mount Misery before the Hall is closed and the gate is locked for the night. However, if you park here, you will have a bit of a hike back to Sweet Hollow Road to access the south trails of the nature preserve.

During one of our many adventures to Mount Misery, Diane and I hiked to a small cemetery hidden in the forest with local woods expert Laurie Farber, founder and executive director of Starflower Experiences, a children's environmental learning group that met in Sweet Hollow Hall at the time. Laurie often led groups of children into the woods of the nature preserve for learning expeditions through which they could gain hands-on experiences with the trees, plants, flowers, and view the wildlife in a natural setting. On this day, when we went on the trails of Mount Misery, Laurie was armed with a detailed map of the area that she had secured from the Long Island Orienteering Club. Our small group parked at Sweet Hollow Hall, but we had to walk a half-mile or so back to Sweet Hollow Road and then cut south along the road and then onto a parallel trail to get to other trails that climbed Mount Misery.

We were in search of the small historic Ketcham Family Cemetery situated on the southern slope of Mount Misery, close to the back of houses on a cul-de-sac off Old Country Road. Historians believe the Ketcham family owned a farm on land located just west of the Presbyterian Church of Sweet Hollow on Old Country Road. In the olden days, farming families buried their dead on their own land.

Gated road leading to Sweet Hollow Hall, a Suffolk County-owned facility where people can park and hike in the woods during day hours.

Laurie said the way she was bringing us to the cemetery was the best way she knew to get to there, and she was right, it was the only way at the time. However, it was a hard journey, cutting through rugged brush and dangerous terrain where trails were not available. Since then, though, an old path has been cleared behind the Presbyterian Church of Sweet Hollow at 95 Old Country Road that takes hikers a short distance east to the little graveyard, so they don't have to hike through the rough, prickly woods. Parking at and accessing the graveyard from the Presbyterian Church, however, is not permitted.

The road that leads to Sweet Hollow Hall (pictured above). It begins where Gwynne Road ends at the intersection of Sweet Hollow Road.

I called the office of Rev. Rebecca Lynne Segers at the Presbyterian Church of Sweet Hollow to ask about the church's stance on strangers parking in the church lot to access the Ketcham Family Cemetery. I had previously spoken to her in 2008, at which time she expressed a favorable attitude towards people visiting the cemetery and had not indicated any opposition to these same people parking in the church lot. She even mentioned at the time how church members had volunteered to clean brush away on the trail near the church so people could more readily access the Huntington Town Historic Cemetery.

However, when I called in late July 2011 to speak with Rev. Segers, I couldn't get past her secretary, who immediately grew terse when I mentioned that my partner and I write books about ghosts. The conversation went straight downhill. She said, "I'll be right back." In the few minutes that I was kept waiting, I heard loud voices in the background. When she returned, she did not even address my wish to speak with Rev. Segers. Instead, she said the following, word-for-word: "Reverend Segers said, 'We don't believe in ghosts. We don't want unauthorized vehicles or people on church property. We don't want people parking here.'"

According to Huntington Town maps, a right-of-way to the cemetery is supposed to exist from Country Meadow Court, the aforementioned cul-de-sac, located between the church and Sweet Hollow Road, on the north side of Old Country Road, but somehow that right-of-way seems to have been eaten up by the private property of a home or homes, some of which have dogs that bark at hikers in the nearby woods, alarming local residents of visitors in the neighborhood. Loose dogs are an additional good reason not to visit the cemetery at night. Getting frightened by a dog in the middle of the dark night could lead to panic and panic could lead to injury or a fatality in these dangerous woods.

Wherever you park — anywhere in the area — make sure you check all parking signage to make sure it's legal. If you park in the dirt spots in front of the West Hills Nature Preserve entrance at night, expect the possibility of police looking inside the woods for you. There was a big fire in these woods a few years ago and ten acres of land were scorched. You can understand why the police might be jumpy.

Also, don't be surprised if you bump into other small groups of thrill seekers who wander into the woods for brief spells. Usually these visitors are teenagers having a little ghost-hunting fun. They typically don't go deep into the woods and they usually don't stay in the woods for more time than it takes to have a cursory glance around. Very often they make a lot of noise. The girls among them often scream and the boys tend to shout obscenities. When they drive in the area, these same kids often speed, turn off their headlights and cut car engines in the middle of the road, shout, and honk horns. These visitors are exactly the kind of obnoxious people local residents don't want around their neck of the woods because such people disrupt the peace and quiet of the neighborhood and cause hazards for everyone.

Supposedly, in recent years, out-of-town gangs have taken a liking to the woods off Sweet Hollow Road. Though we have never seen them, or evidence of them, other people who have heard of these gangs have described their members as violent. We have never met anybody who has had a first-hand experience with these reputed gangs, but it's something to think about when considering your personal safety.

The Overpass

A little farther north from the preserve's entrance is the overpass that carries vehicles on the Northern State Parkway across Sweet Hollow Road. Strangely, this overpass is located right in the heart of the woods. Visitors do not actually see the cars traveling across the overpass, but they can hear the whirling of car tires against the pavement overhead. Sometimes the tires sound like voices whispering secrets. People often report hearing children singing and laughing in the wide tunnel below the bridge.

The cursed woods of Sweet Hollow Road were given the name West Hills Nature Preserve in 1974 by Suffolk County Legislature's Resolution #666, so, right off the bat, the 174-acre preserve was associated with evil in many people's thinking. According to the Bible's Book of Revelation, "666" is the number of the "beast."

> "Here is wisdom. Let him that hath understanding count the number of the beast: for it is the number of a man; and his number is six hundred threescore and six."

Is "666" a coincidence or a clue about what lies in-wait in these forsaken woods? After all, the 666 woods of West Hills Nature Preserve blanket infamously haunted Mt. Misery, where so many paranormal events have been reported (see next chapter). Sweet Hollow Road, like Mount Misery itself, abounds with reports of ghosts and aberrations of the night. Many people speak of awful screaming in the woods. These are the same woods that roll down the Mount to the godforsaken snake that is Sweet Hollow Road. All three places — Sweet Hollow Road, Mt. Misery, and the road that runs across the top of it, Mt. Misery Road — are geographically interconnected. All three places are believed to be conduits for beings from other dimensions.

Don't be surprised if you feel sick or you find that you cannot concentrate properly when you visit the snake's tail of the Haunted Mile of Sweet Hollow Road. People have reported feeling light-headed, confused, and cold while at this location. Many people get outright feverish and end up out-of-commission for a week or more.

People also report being touched, hit, and having their cameras, voice recorders, cell phones, or walkie-talkies grabbed from their hands at this place of dark wonder. Likewise, visitors complain of having their hats knocked off their heads while in the woods. Cold spots and paranormal "cobwebs" are also commonly experienced here.

Some people we interviewed claimed they felt depressed for weeks or months following their visits to the road. Others said they developed colds, bronchitis, pneumonia, and strange aches and pains following their visits.

Many people swear to never return to Sweet Hollow because they believe it's a gathering point for Evil.

Sweet Hollow Road Legends

Mary

There are many legends associated with Sweet Hollow Road, one of which is about the ghost of Mary, Long Island's most infamous and hideous witch.

Mary is not a nature-loving witch like those of modern day, but more the kind of witch that witch hunters concocted descriptions of during the Spanish Inquisition, the kind accused of eating children like the witch in the story of "Hansel and Gretel," the kind of witch that is reputed to be in the same league with the Devil himself. Personally, I've never met a witch that matches this description — and I've met quite a few.

Supposedly, Mary, the dreadful witch of old Sweet Hollow Valley, was burned at the stake in the woods at dusk by the townspeople with yellow hay torches because she set fire to the little red schoolhouse with black shutters and which was occupied by screaming children whom she had locked inside. The flames shot out orange, red, and yellow against the pink and auburn autumn sky. The screaming was awful, it's said, like metal twisting. Horses in barns three miles away kicked their way out of their stalls and all the birds of the area left for days. It's said a lone turkey vulture was seen hovering the area for a week; such a bird, the legends point out, is not natural to this environment.

A variation of the terrible legend says Mary burned down a brick hospital filled with patients and staff clambering desperately at the hard plaster walls to get out. She barred the handles of the doors with the local church's crucifixes so her victims couldn't leave. Outside the doors she stood and laughed.

Some versions claim the hospital she burned down was really a miserably decrepit insane asylum where Mary was a patient. In this version of the legend, she enjoyed killing the doctors and nurses and even took her time. They shouldn't have asked her so many questions and been so insulting! They also should have locked up the shed where they kept the hatchets and axes.

In all the legends the building that was burned down was located on a high point on Mt. Misery Road. Some people we have spoken to think it might have been where the brown utility pole now stands at the northwest corner of the intersection of Old Country and Mount Misery Roads.

Mary's angry spirit is said to now wander bleak Sweet Hollow Road, Mt. Misery, and Mt. Misery Road. Beware: Mary is seeking revenge. She has sworn her allegiance to Satan and now hungrily seeks out souls to drag down to hell with her... Such are the legends. We will tell more of the shocking story of Mary later in the chapter about Mount Misery. We can only hope reading these legends will not inspire you to dream about black beings with red eyes and large bat wings standing at the edge of your bed at night like we have heard they do. Going deep into the legends bring some people down a dark road that you may not want to venture, lest you grow more intimate with Melville, the man who took Mary from the ball in the mansion that snowy Halloween night.

We are not saying the ghost of Mary is not real or trying to invalidate people's experiences — especially alien dreams — but our research concluded there was never a schoolhouse or a hospital on Mount Misery Road. Some people don't like to hear this because they want to believe the schoolhouse or a hospital really burned down with people inside it. It makes the story of Mary despicably foul, but evermore beefy with much drama and horrible tragedy to imagine.

Meanwhile, where Mary's angry ghost will show up next is the burning question. The answer is anybody's guess. Ghost hunters often feel Mary's malignant presence beside them in the dusky woods while they investigate, especially on full-moon nights and Halloween night.

It must be remembered these are county-owned woods and no one is allowed in county parklands after dark. Because the police are aware of ghost hunters in the area, they might be more apt to fine, or possibly arrest, violators if discovered at night in the woods — especially if the ghost hunters are behaving inappropriately by lighting fires, being loud, or partying. The potential for police action against violators of the sanctity of the county woods is something to think about before jumping out of a car on the spur of the moment at night and running into the woods to see ghosts.

Ghost enthusiasts have all day to research in the parklands legally, right up to dusk. It takes a knowledgeable, well-equipped, and well-intentioned ghost investigator to successfully plan and execute a nighttime investigation in the woods of Sweet Hollow without drawing attention from the local residents or getting hurt. Few investigators we know actually conduct nighttime investigations in the woods of Sweet Hollow and most of them avoid this place altogether, chiefly because it's just plain unsafe to be tramping around a parkland at night.

However, researchers relate that they can sense and even see Mary's malicious energy in the dark of the night or sometimes even smell her sulfur odor. Usually this is the point when less robust investigators grab their equipment and make a fast escape out of the woods to go home to their safe beds, most likely to dream about hellish creatures with claws and large dripping teeth staring at their necks while they sleep, unable to move.

Many people have experienced Mary's wrath in one way or another. One man we interviewed said he saw his friend — a young lady in his group of inexperienced ghost seekers — mysteriously trip and fall while walking on Sweet Hollow Road. Immediately following the fall the young lady was dragged backwards by her hair into the woods by a disembodied entity, he claimed.

The witness alleged the girl fought an invisible force while screaming for help. Meanwhile, neither the witness nor anybody else in his group could understand what was going on because only the young lady could see the foul hag with the black shawl over her head that was ripping out her hair. The hag screamed black curses at her, but nobody but the girl could hear them. The hag was a demon from hell, the witness said.

The witnesses to the atrocity against the young girl could see the girl's hair standing straight out, as if wrapped in an invisible hand, dragging the girl away from her friends and into the gloomy trees of the foreboding forest, presumably to kill in some disgusting manner. Said Frank Greco of Franklin Square: "Her hair was standing straight out! I couldn't see nothing. We had to cut her hair with a scissor to get her loose!"

The Ghost Bride

Another of the more disturbing legends of Sweet Hollow Road is that of the ghost bride, also known as The Lady in White, that appears in headlights at the sides of the road or is sometimes witnessed crossing Sweet Hollow Road. Apparently, she wanders the dense, dark night not knowing she is dead.

In headlights, the ghost bride appears forlorn and lost. She is caught in an endless cycle of searching for her lost life.

It's said the Lady in White appears in a wedding dress, for she died on the very night of her wedding. Some people believe the dead bride was killed in a car accident, for the road is twisted and dangerous and has claimed other lives over the years, while other people say the bride was murdered on her wedding night, maybe by her jealous husband.

Other people believe the Lady in White of Sweet Hollow Road is not a bride at all, but the ghost of a woman wearing the same flowing gown in which she was buried after she died in some unknown way.

While not claiming it was the ghost of the bride or the ghost of Mary, psychic Barbara Loiko of Farmingdale said she saw the apparition of a woman many times while driving up and down Sweet Hollow Road, usually at dusk, to and from a farm on nearby Old Country Road, where she worked.

"She looked as though she was waiting for someone," remembered Loiko.

The spot where Loiko saw the woman was usually the same, on the east side of Sweet Hollow Road, just a few hundred feet south of the Northern State Parkway overpass — the side of the bridge that is closest to Route 110.

Loiko described the ghost as looking like a "Gibson Girl," a woman of proper social behavior and style from the early part of the twentieth century. The ghost's hair was always in a bun and she wore a blouse with a high collar. High collars were the fashion familiar to stylish woman of that period.

"She looked so alone, so lost," recalled Loiko. "She looked like she was waiting for someone — just waiting. So sad."

The Suicide Teenagers

Most visitors to Sweet Hollow Road seem particularly fascinated with a legend they believe actually carries built-in instructions on how to conjure some of the ghosts of the road.

Thrill seekers often shut down their vehicles after placing the shifters in neutral and beep their horns three times while under, or just before, the Northern State Parkway overpass that crosses Sweet Hollow Road. It is believed that performing this very dangerous ritual conjures the ghosts of three teenagers who hanged themselves from the overpass in fulfillment of a bizarre suicide pact. Our in-depth research has shown no teenagers ever hanged themselves from this overpass.

Some people also claim a bus filled with children somehow crashed at the overpass in the 1930s and all the children died. This tragedy, they say, produced ghosts believed to push vehicles in neutral gear against gravity through the tunnel to safety. It's assumed the ghost children push the vehicles because many people claim they find tiny fingerprints and small handprints on the bumpers, trunk doors, and rear windows of their vehicles following experiences of being pushed through the tunnel.

While a train did collide with a bus filled with school children in California in the 1930s, killing the children, the legend associated with the overpass on Sweet Hollow Road can't be true because the overpass wasn't even built until the mid-1940s. Therefore, no school bus filled with children collided under the bridge in the 1930s. Moreover, there are no reports of this accident in newspaper archives.

However, so many people have experienced this phenomenon of having their cars pushed by unseen hands that it's useless trying to argue sense with them. Even when it's pointed out that the road is not level under overpass, people will still argue that what they experienced is true — that they really were pushed uphill by spirits!

This problem is reminiscent of an excellent episode of the Syfy Channel's television program, *Fact or Faked: Paranormal Files*, a show in which clever investigators employ tools used by land surveyors to solve a mystery.

The riddle was that vehicles placed in neutral just before a railroad crossing appeared to roll uphill against gravity on their own accord. These vehicles would climb the apparent incline and cross the railroad tracks where legend had it children were killed in a school bus by a speeding train many years ago. However, after the show's researchers employed the surveying tools to the puzzle, it was found that what was actually going on was a case of optical illusion.

Though people were suggesting the ghosts of the dead children in a school bus accident from long ago were pushing vehicles over railroad tracks to help them escape being hit by a train, investigators found that the road only appeared to climb upwards, when in fact, it sank in a decline.

The school bus that investigators borrowed for the show, and put in neutral just before the tracks, rolled up the apparent incline on its own because gravity was pulling it down. The road only looked like it was climbing up towards the tracks because the land at the side of the road created an effect whereby the road, too, appeared to be at an incline. The road, meanwhile, took an imperceptible dip. Thus the bus moved on its own over the tracks as the result. It didn't look or feel right to local investigators who believed that the road went up, but facts are facts, and the bus rolled in neutral because the road angled downwards at that spot.

So, who's pushing the vehicles uphill at Sweet Hollow Road? Is it the teenagers who never hanged themselves there, the dead bus children who never died there, or some other ghost such as Mary or the Lady in White who probably was never killed there?

Is gravity pulling vehicles through the tunnel of the overpass?

Is it something else? Something we don't understand? Something truly paranormal?

Answer: It's gravity!

Caution: Drivers should never stop their cars under the overpass, especially at night. Drivers speed madly on this crazy road. Stopping on Sweet Hollow Road at the overpass or anywhere else could cause a fatal accident.

Some people say drivers on Sweet Hollow Road typically drive irrationally because the spirits take charge of their senses and make them place themselves and other people in danger. Whatever the cause, speeding or turning off your car while on this road could transform you from a visitor to the road to its next legend. You could kill yourself and other people by acting stupidly on this most dangerous of roads. Be smart and be safe!

One other caution: Police patrol Sweet Hollow Road regularly. Residents in the area complain frequently of beeping horns at the overpass at all hours of the night, yelling and screaming, speeding, littering, and other disturbing behavior on the part of visitors looking for ghosts. Diane and I have been pulled over many times on this road; officers have told us local residents are fed up with obnoxious people who don't belong in the neighborhood, so if you venture up Sweet Hollow Road, stay within the law and don't go in the woods after dark. Considering all the spirits — alive and dead — that might have a bone to pick with you, it's best to heed this warning.

The Ghouls of Mt. Misery & Other Creatures

LOCATION: The expansive landscape of Mt. Misery is sliced in two parts by the Northern State Parkway, creating two separate areas known as Mt. Misery: A south area, south of the Parkway, and a north area, north of the parkway.

DIRECTIONS: There are many access points to Mount Misery. The entranceway we recommend is through Sweet Hollow Road's woods up onto the Mount, for the woods of the flat land along Sweet Hollow Road cover the base of Mount Misery. For any other access points, you should consult a map of the county parklands.

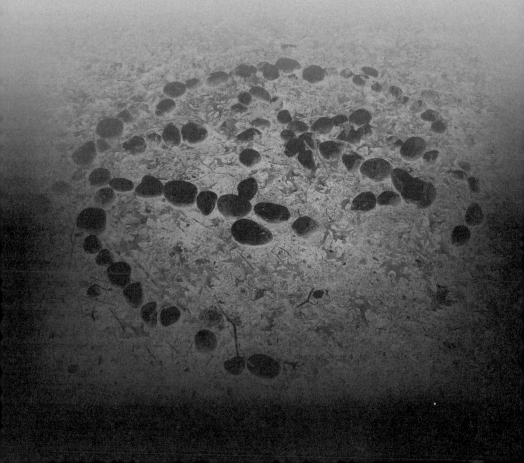

Dark Mount Misery in Melville is haunted place that is inhospitable and unknowable.

The Mount is a place of old Indian trails and frightening legends that were handed down through the generations from as far back as its settlers in the mid-1600s. Many of its later settlers (1690s) came from Salem, Massachusetts. Salem was the despicable town where the witch trials took place in 1692; nineteen people were hanged and one person was crushed to death for being witches.

One frightening story from Sweet Hollow, known as The Fiddler's Tale, is that of Mary. It's said a tall, thin gentleman in fine black clothing, dragging a clubbed-foot behind him as he walked and carrying a finely polished black cane with a vein of real gold running through it, arrived to a community ball at the finest house in the valley. He pulled up in a thundering, shiny, black carriage pulled by six coal-black steeds and driven by a little blue man in a top hat. It's said the early October snow parted before the carriage as it pulled up. The snow melted on the steps of the mansion before the gentleman as he climbed the staircase with wheezes and grunts to the door of the house.

All the young and beautiful women of the valley swooned and the men froze like statues as the gentleman went straight for the most lovely of the young ladies in the room, whose name was Mary. She fell into the gentleman's arms and he swept her up without so much as a word as to who he was or what he was going to do with her.

Mary was not seen again for years. When she was, she was a wicked woman who burned down a school with children in it. When she was caught, the angry people of Ketcham's Hollow, the old name for Sweet Hollow, burned her at the stake in the woods of Mount Misery, possibly at a dead tree that once existed at the intersection of Old Country and Mount Misery roads, where a brown telephone pole now stands and is marked by the stenciled words "Mt. Misery Rd."

Mary's laughter filled the woods as if she could not even feel the scorching tongues of yellow and red flames licking her melting flesh. She screamed to the entire valley that she would come back to exact the Devil's due. "Even your children's children and their grandchildren will see me! They will pay the price for what you've done today!"

Now, seemingly true to her words, her spirit seeks revenge. It's said she's an earthbound entity in the woods where she was burned alive.

Of course, that's just a legend. Right?

Not to the fiddler who was playing with other musicians at the ball in the mansion in Sweet Hollow Valley on the snowy night poor Mary was abducted. He recounted the dark story for years as he made the rounds in rural Long Island hamlets, playing the fiddle in lusty taverns where ale spilled on the floors, men arm-wrestled in the corners, and women danced with each other and bickered at their men for flirting with younger girls. People gathered around the burning fireplace with eyes wide upon him and ears tuned to his every word. A hush would fall over the place, and even the stout tavern keepers would put down their white towels and listen. "Tell us the story of Mary," the women often called to the fiddler, who had many stories to tell about Mount Misery.

"Ole Jack," as he was called, would smile — a tall, thin man, he was, with a hungry look about him — and grab up a squeaky wooden chair and pull it along the brown boards of the creaking splintery floor into the center of the crowd, with his brown eyes gleaming, and his round, worn black hat placed upside down on the floor beside him for tips, which always came aplenty. The candles would flicker in his eyes.

The fiddler's tale has been pieced together with fragments gathered here and there from people we interviewed, with a dash of writer's magic to help all the pieces fit together. In the end, of course, it's more tale and legend than fact.

Remember, some of the settlers of the area came to Sweet Hollow from Salem, Massachusetts, home of the deadly witch trials of 1692. Why did they escape from Salem? What infections of the mind and spirit did they bring with them to Sweet Hollow? Were they guilty of putting innocent people to death by claiming they were witches? Were they witches themselves? Could their social distortions be responsible for the troubles stirring on Sweet Hollow Road and in the woods of Mount Misery today? Or were the early settlers of Sweet Hollow innocents who wanted to escape the evil of Salem and were followed out of Massachusetts by the Devil himself?

Many members of the hard-working farmers who settled the area might be buried without markers in a small graveyard hidden deep in the woods on Mount Misery's slope, forever sealing away the secrets of what happened in this place that makes it so miserable and so haunted.

While graves in the old Ketcham Family Cemetery with the name "Mary" can be found in this historic graveyard — officially containing thirty-one graves that researchers from the Town of Huntington were able to find — it's highly unlikely any of these women were the Mary of the terrible legends.

It's said Mount Misery is a place twisted in mystery and locked inside the impenetrable darkness of the paranormal. Visitors often complain of having been lured into a mind-set of fear on the Mount, later dreaming of black beings and winged entities they claim visit them in their rooms at night. Other people claim to get sick in the woods. Some people find themselves drawn to Evil afterwards.

One woman from Farmingdale told us after one of our lectures that she saw her dead neighbor, whom she had never spoken with, floating over her bed when she opened her eyes on the night he died. "I didn't know he had died till days later, so it's not like I had prior knowledge," the woman began. "I quickly closed my eyes, but when I opened them again, he was still there! This time he was made of all black shadows and had large black wings like a bat's. His mouth was open in an "O." I knew he was telling me he was dead." This occurred on the night of her first and only visit to Mount Misery looking for ghosts. "I will never go back there again!" the woman said. "Never!"

Above left: A pentangle of white stones inside a circle, probably disturbed by an animal, was found in the woods of West Hills Nature Preserve on Mount Misery by paranormal investigator R. L. Demri of Central Islip. This Satanic symbol may have been arranged on the ground by true Satanists who meet secretly in the woods at night, or by teenagers acting out their "stoner" fancies. **Above right:** Joseph Flammer examines the remains of a fire in the woods in an area where signs of nighttime gatherings or meetings are sometimes found. The beer bottle next to Joseph's foot indicates the fire was probably enjoyed by teenagers drinking in the woods rather than by occultists. Most groups that are known to hold religious rituals in the woods are highly respectful of the environment and leave no signs they were ever there.

On the map, Mount Misery is a rectangle. Its scraggly trees climb a hill up and away from Sweet Hollow Road. The Mount elevates to one of the highest points on Long Island. It was formed by the ice age many thousands of years ago.

An observer would be more nearly correct to call Mount Misery a hill rather than a Mount, short for "mountain." After all, it's less than four hundred feet tall and, although many of us are familiar with the neatly packaged explanations of why the Mount is called "Misery" — that the settlers of Sweet Hollow Valley found it misery to get their mules and horses and wagons up and over the hill's tall incline — we can't help but remember Occam's razor, a law of economics that states the simplest explanation is usually the correct one. In this case, the reason why the Mount got the name "Misery" is because misery flowed down the hill's slope and spilled into the world, bringing entities from hell to the front doors of residents in Sweet Hollow. One must merely recall the man with the cane and top hat who took Mary away to infamy.

Sweet Hollow was the name for the hamlet down in the valley at the base of Mount Misery before it was called Melville, though its original name was Samuel Ketcham's Hollow. It's believed the Hollow was settled before 1668. It's more than likely Sweet Hollow got its name from farmers, who, once they escaped the Mount's intense paranormal misery, got down the hill, perhaps kissing the ground, exclaiming, "Sweet Hollow!" Historians, of course, say that the Hollow was called "Sweet" on account of the honey found in trees in the area. Nobody knows why Sweet Hollow was later called Melville, though it has been suggested the man who took Mary away was known only as Melville.

Three tribes of Indians lived on the land: the Matinecock, Secatogue, and Massapequa. According to documents supplied by Huntington Historical Society, "Old Country Road was the Indian path that divided the tribes."

Mount Misery's borders are wide. Bill Knell, an author, television and radio program host, and UFO researcher, wrote expert articles about Mount Misery, saying in part:

> "Manetto Hill Road is the western border, while Walt Whitman Road borders the Mount on the eastern side. Mount Misery begins just off of Old Country Road on its southern side and ends at Jericho Turnpike to the north. Although it's only a little over a mile in distance end to end in any direction, a lot of history is packed into that mile and not all of it is the kind you want to see taught in school."

Privately, I have heard knowledgeable paranormal investigators refer to Mount Misery as "The Dungeon," for they suggest that what dwells within its dingy walls of sun-flecked trees screams out in pain at night and makes itself evident — in one way or anther, eventually — to the Mount's visitors who go looking for it.

Sometimes misty ghosts appear like dancing mirages in the solid black night. Sometimes balls of light, known as ghost lights, flare red, blue, and white amid the trees like orphaned spirits looking for a way home. Other times lights appear like falling stars from out of the sky. Some witnesses have suggested the lights are from extraterrestrial crafts hovering silver and ominous over the trees in the oppressive midnight or from black ops. military helicopters searching for extraterrestrials and unearthly predators stalking the woods.

Off the Mount's beaten trails the dull shades of green glinting off the leaves of scraggly trees and thorny bushes offer up a gloom that is pronounced even on the sunniest of days. The terrain is largely rugged with uncooperative brush. The environment here lacks charm. In fact, people often say they feel uncomfortable in these woods; it is as if they are being watched by eyes hidden amongst the trees. Often these same people find themselves anxious to get out of the woods — and fast.

What happens on Mount Misery is typically profoundly personal and persuasive. Like children who play with fire, visitors to Mount Misery tend to remember what they experienced here and avoid the place in the future: You get burned once, you don't want to get burned again. This includes many ghost hunters we interviewed who have either gotten sick on the Mount or felt they were visited by evil spirits afterwards.

As early as 2004, people were writing to me and Diane telling us of their awful experiences in the Mount's woods. Mitchell Rakoff, for example, was a fellow ghost hunter I corresponded with during the days when he, Diane, and I were in the same Long Island ghost hunting group. Mitchell wrote in an e-mail: "First off, Joe, me and Sweet Hollow don't get along very well. I went with a friend and...I got bronchitis for well over three months. Something apparently got into me and I guess wanted to teach me a lesson. So I got my lumps out of that one, not so sweet for me!" Mitchell said he would never go back there.

Mount Misery's attitude discourages wandering alone far from the established trails. A hiker never knows where a deep hole or a wasp nest might be in the brush or if there might be a rotted Indian grave that is about to cave in under ages of fallen leaves littered with sticks and ancient Long Island mystery.

Nor does one know when he or she might come face-to-face with a legendary red-eyed entity towering eight feet tall with a wingspan sixteen-feet wide, which people have actually claimed to seen. Keep reading.

Many paranormal enthusiasts have told us they believe Mount Misery is a portal to "the other side," but in this case, the other side includes more than just ghosts and monsters, it includes extraterrestrials and beings from the bowels of other dimensions that we can't even begin to fathom without first understanding such complex phenomena as worm holes, black holes, and parallel universes. We need to understand the inter-dimensional universe and the extra-dimensional universe, both of which are incomprehensible. Such understanding may not ever be within mankind's grasp.

We must be clear that the area of Mount Misery we are talking about does not include residential sections on the Mount or on Old Country Road, the little road that climbs the Mount from Sweet Hollow Road to Mount Misery Road, or even a few commercial facilities that are in the area, some of which border the woods. Rather, we are talking exclusively about the woods. To this day, we have never had a homeowner from the communities on Mount Misery contact us to complain about paranormal activity, and those who we spoke with deny there is any paranormal activity at all, placing the inspiration for legends of ghosts, ghouls, monsters, and extraterrestrials on foolhardy, gullible ghost enthusiasts.

We'll see.

Paranormal investigators John Snow, George Mendoza, Brigid Goode, and Michele Snow stand at the gate to a small family graveyard on the slope of Mount Misery in West Hills Nature Preserve. The Town of Huntington counted thirty-one graves in this overgrown graveyard, but there could be many more here that are not represented by markers.

Miseries on the Mount

Though ghost stories abound about Mount Misery, it is its stories of UFOs, extraterrestrials, Men in Black, and monsters that most people know best, thanks to investigator John A. Keel, who authored the 1975 book *The Mothman Prophecies*, which gained widespread attention when it was released as a movie starring Richard Gere and Laura Linney in 2002. The movie, however, was barely recognizable as the story in the book. Previously Keel had written the 1970 book *Strange Creatures from Time and Space*.

Sadly, Keel died in 2009 before Diane and I could visit him at his home in Manhattan and gain access to his most private files about Mount Misery, which, we suspect, were kept in a locked file cabinet or vault because releasing them would have caused widespread public fear about the possibility of invasion by other beings. In the end, what we have available to us are his published texts.

In *Mothman*, Keel suddenly diverts our attention away from his all-important investigation of sightings of a winged creature in Point Pleasant, West Virginia, in 1966 and 1967, to discuss strange happenings many hundreds of miles away on Mount Misery, Long Island. Here is what he said on the history of the place:

> "For decades, the Mount was known as a haunted place, the site of a number of mysterious deaths and disappearances. In the spring of 1967, young couples necking on the back roads began to see low-flying UFOs, particularly around a field that was used as a junk yard for old cars. Others claimed to see a giant hairy monster with gleaming red eyes."

Further, in a nineteen-page chapter titled "Misery on the Mount," Keel tells us about Men in Black (MIB) who visited Mount Misery. Keel did not even pretend to understand why they appeared on Long Island.

In this case, the MIBs were not like those in the 1997 movie *Men in Black* starring Tommy Lee Jones and Will Smith. In the movie *Men in Black*, the MIBs were government agents out to stop silly extraterrestrials from destroying the Earth. This characterization of Men in Black is actually a distortion of Keel's "Men in Black," who he identified as extraterrestrials or extra-dimensional beings that imitate humans while among us. These fakes typically had sharp Oriental features, black eyes, often wore black clothing, sometimes drove black Cadillacs, and almost always seemed to have no experience effectively imitating human beings.

In fact, the extraterrestrials, or inter-dimensional beings, that Keel labeled as MIBs in his book had problems talking and walking correctly; and minor everyday items that humans don't even stop to think about fascinated the MIBs and made them gleeful. In one case, an MIB was so fascinated with a common cheap plastic pen that he could barely keep his thoughts on the conversation at hand with a human he visited for some strange purpose. When the human gave him the pen to keep, the MIB acted as if he had won the lottery and showed it off to the other MIBs he was with.

Why extraterrestrials were even visiting Mount Misery, or Point Pleasant, is never fully grasped by Keel. In the end, he suggested that the Mothman, Men in Black, UFOs, and extraterrestrials might actually be diversions to keep humans from noticing a larger plot being carried out by inter-dimensional beings right under our noses. The raging phenomenon of Point Pleasant, for example, was just to keep attention away from a larger truth. What the real plot perpetrated by inter-dimensional beings might have been, or might still be, he couldn't say.

This lack of understanding of the paranormal and inter-dimensional beings seems applicable for Long Islanders when considering Mount Misery and its mysteries.

Probably the best known story Keel told of Mt. Misery is that of four men, who, in April 1967, visited an old woman who lived alone near the summit. The strange men appeared right after a severe rainstorm. Three of the men were well dressed, the other shabbily dressed. Keel recorded his conversation with the old lady whom the MIBs had visited:

> "'They had high cheekbones and very red faces, like a bad sunburn,' she told me. 'They were very polite, but they said my land belonged to their tribe and they were going to get it back. What frightened me was their feet. They didn't have a car...they must have walked up that muddy hill...but their shoes were spotlessly clean. There was no trace of mud or water where they walked in my house.'"

In the same week, another visitor showed up at the woman's house on Mount Misery:

> "This one was a woman with striking white hair who claimed to represent a local newspaper. She carried a book like 'a big ledger' and asked the witness a number of personal questions about her family background.

When I later checked with the newspaper, I found they employed no one of that description."

Another story Keel told in *Mothman* was about a woman he named "Jane." With her boyfriend Richard, Jane visited Mount Misery at night to see if they could witness some of the strange lights and UFOs people had been seeing in the area. Many of these people had called-in their sightings to a WBAB radio show hosted by Miss Jaye P. Paro; Keel tells us Paro was a Mount Misery expert. According to Keel, lines of cars filled with people visited the Mount during this time for the same reason — to see UFOs.

However, as it turned out, on this night, Jane and Richard strayed from the other thrill seekers and drifted around the Mount on their own, at last coming near High Hold, the old Henry Stimson estate on the summit. Richard, at this point, said he felt sick and slumped over the steering wheel unconscious. Here's what Keel wrote about what followed:

> "Jane was terrified, but before she could focus her attention on him, a brilliant beam of light shot out of the woods 'like a floodlight.' It dazzled her and she fell back in her seat unable to move.
>
> "The next thing they knew they were driving along Old Country Road at the base of Mount Misery.
>
> "'How did we get here?' Richard asked her, baffled. 'What happened?'
>
> "'Let's go home,' Jane choked."

Jane's experiences with the bizarreness of Mount Misery had only just begun, though. Following the incident with the bright light in the woods, Jane was contacted on the telephone by a "metallic voice" that instructed her to go to a local library and look up a certain book on Indian history. (This library is probably Half Hollow Hills Library, located on Sweet Hollow Road, the very library Diane and I have conducted research at on many occasions.)

When Jane entered the library, a woman dressed in 1940s period clothing seemed to expect her and handed her a book. Jane immediately read the book, which contained a message just for her. The words on the page expanded and shrunk as she read them. Afterwards, she was sick, vomiting, for a few days. Later, the 1940s library woman showed up unexpectedly at strange places and delivered to Jane even stranger messages. One such message was, "Peter's coming." Another time Jane found herself in a trance when MIBs in a black Cadillac pulled over and talked with her.

During that period of time, Keel explained, there was a woman who called herself Princess Moon Owl who told Long Islanders over Miss Paro's WBAB radio program that she was from the planet Ceres and that she was 350 years old. "I am from another planet," she told eager listeners. "I came here by flying saucer."

Monsters in the Woods?

In an article that appeared in *Beyond* magazine in July 1969, a witness actually produced a photograph of a long-nailed, human-like creature mopped in dark hair or rags. The photo was supposedly shot on Mount Misery at 8 a.m. on a Sunday morning in January 1969 by Miss Jaye P. Paro, the Mt. Misery expert and radio show host.

The story goes that Miss Paro and two friends were scouting Mount Misery on foot that Sunday morning when suddenly the beast appeared from out of the trees and approached the unsuspecting group. The creature took a look at the three hikers and reached a hand out towards Paro as she took its photograph — and then the beast turned back to the woods to vanish forever among the trees.

One of the witnesses who was hiking with Miss Paro that day described the creature in *Strange Creatures from Time and Space* as "something that resembled a human, disfigured face, long wild black hair, and dressed in a long black garment." The photo is admittedly fuzzy and even Keel referred to the creature as a "black blob" because of the poor quality of the black and white photograph.

Nonetheless, the creature appears to be low to the ground with one hand outstretched towards the photographer. From the photograph it is very clear that the creature has white skin and five digits on the outstretched hand. Moreover, it appears that its thumb is an opposable thumb like a human's and unlike the thumbs of other primates, which have thumbs more turned away from their other fingers. Lastly, although the image makes it appear the creature is using its hands to walk like an ape, it also appears the creature's outstretched hand is clean, free of mud and dirt. More than likely, this creature did not really use its hands to walk. It's also more than likely, the creature was human... so what are we to think of this alleged monster?

This drawing is not far off from the description of the strange creature that appeared to hikers in the woods of Mount Misery on a Sunday morning in January 1969 and was photographed by Jaye P. Paro: it was published, with an accompanying article, in *Beyond*, a national magazine, in July 1969. *Drawing by Karen Isaksen*.

Obviously, there are only a few choices. The creature is either a hideous fake, part of a great farce that Keel and his friends launched to fool believers of strange creatures and monsters. Or the creature was real, perhaps a manifestation of death, a ghost, a shade from the grave, or even more likely, a ghoul. Given the many reports of paranormal activity on the Mount, it would be wise to be slow in dismissing Miss Paro's creature without at least considering the possibilities of it being real. Take a look at the photo on the website www.johnkeel.com/?p=246 and judge for yourself.

Those of us who have investigated the woods of Mt. Misery know the feeling of having something following us through the night, even causing noises of footfalls and shuffles that stop when we stop on the trails to listen.

Miseries on the Mount II

In our days of investigating Sweet Hollow Road and the woods of Mount Misery, we have met no investigators more knowledgeable about the ghosts therein — or more persistent in finding them — than Long Island ghost investigators Kevin Kelly of Massapequa Park, William (Bill) Berongi of Massapequa Park, and Keith Baecker of Roslyn Heights. They are members of the small but elite ghost hunting group Long Island Paranormal Seekers (LIPS) and are truly experts when it comes to paranormal phenomena on Sweet Hollow Road and Mount Misery because they have lived it. Diane and I consult these researchers when we need to know more about certain matters on the Mount and Sweet Hollow Road because they have seen it all.

The investigators of LIPS have spent many nights out in the woods of Sweet Hollow Road and upper Mount Misery, sometimes till near dawn. This may be considered extreme ghost hunting by many people, but these investigators are after the truth about paranormal activity in the woods and they choose to pursue their goal zealously.

Kevin, Bill, and Keith are hard-core paranormal investigators with professional equipment and no-nonsense intentions. They don't make noise, disturb anybody, or pollute. They treat the woods with great respect. They slip in and then slip back out.

The gentlemen of LIPS generally believe the most paranormally active area of Mount Misery is the entrance to the West Hills Nature Preserve on Sweet Hollow Road, a place we, too, have encountered

On another night, Diane and I, and psychic John Altieri of North Babylon, a member of the Babylon Paranormal Group, joined Kevin, Bill, and Keith on the Mount for a late-night investigation. The night was dark but loud with cantankerous teenagers racing by the woods on Sweet Hollow Road at the base of the Mount. The kids screamed obscenities, honked car horns, and, in general, conducted themselves in the kind of ill-humored disorderly fashion that quickly draws 911 complaints by local residents and subsequent visits by police cars with swirling red and blue lights.

While Bill, Diane, and I stayed at an impromptu base station in the woods at a lower area of the Mount, photographing the night for spirits, John Altieri, Kevin, and Keith climbed a sandy path going higher up into the trees, to a spot where the LIPS members had experienced paranormal activity on prior outings. The area they ventured to is a place they call "Jason Road" because it is where their friend Jason was summoned by a disembodied male voice that registered on an EVP.

A nighttime investigation on Mount Misery. In addition to other phenomena that occurred on this night, a camera was yanked out of psychic John Altieri's hand. Pictured above: William Berongi, Diane Hill, John Altieri, Keith Baecker, and Kevin Kelly.

Once high up the Mount and on Jason Road, John Altieri psychically looked around at the dark of night with his psychic's third eye and sensed someone had been murdered in that immediate spot. He also said he felt uncomfortable being in that location any longer. All this time, he later revealed, he was struggling with an invisible entity tugging at his camera, trying to get it out of his hand.

"For a good five minutes I was fighting with this thing I couldn't see," said Altieri. "It kept trying to pull my camera out of my hand. It was a tug of war. I didn't want to acknowledge the entity because I didn't want to give it any energy, so I didn't mention it to anybody else."

According to Altieri, it was at this point that investigator Kevin Kelly reported he was feeling ill, the result of being in a spiritually negative environment. Altieri then got on the walkie-talkie and called the base station, relating to me, Diane, and Bill the disturbing events as they were happening.

"It was while I was talking to you on the walkie-talkie that the entity yanked my camera right out of my hand!" recalled Altieri. "And yes, the camera went flying to the ground!"

The group immediately left the area and returned to base to give a full accounting of the frightening activities that had taken place higher up in the woods. However, one aspect of their experience that they couldn't properly convey was the unsettling feeling of having the spirits encircle them and affect their bodies, even touch them. One must experience that feeling for themselves to know what that feels like. For most people, it's a blessing to never experience this. For ghost investigators like Kevin, Bill, and Keith, it's an occupational hazard.

A Little Girl Ghost Goes Home with an Investigator

The hazardous work was far from over for Kevin, Bill, and Keith, however.

It's every ghost investigator's nightmare to bring home an entity from a haunted location, but this is exactly what happened to Keith following an evening of ghost hunting in the woods of Sweet Hollow Road. Recalls Kevin Kelly:

"It was about midnight when we wrapped up our investigation of Sweet Hollow Road and the woods of Mount Misery and got into Keith's car to go home. In the car was me, Keith, and a friend of mine from work. We were driving south on Route 110 – going home – when we started to hear a girl's voice inside the car. It was the strangest thing because the voice was right inside the car with us!

"I was really tired that night. When I got home I went right to sleep. A little later my wife Barbara woke me up. She said Keith (Baecker) was on the telephone and needed to talk to me. I thought, 'Now, this is an odd time for him to be calling me!'

"When I answered the phone, Keith said, 'She's here with me now.'

"Who is? I asked.

"'The girl from inside my car,' Keith said."

Keith remembered the incident clearly:

"That night when the investigation at Sweet Hollow Road concluded, I was at a red light on Route 110 on the way to drop off Kevin and our friend when we heard laughter and murmuring inside the car. It was so strange because it was a girl's voice. I would say she sounded to be about thirteen or fourteen years old. There was a laugh followed by muttering, but we couldn't make out what was said because it was unclear. We didn't have the radio on, and it wasn't any of us laughing or talking, so we looked at each other and wondered what it was we were hearing?

"We were freaked and we talked about the girl's laughter for the rest of the ride to Kevin's house, to drop him off.

"After I dropped off the other two, I was on Wantagh Parkway near the Southern State Parkway on my way home and I heard laughing in the car again. I wasn't afraid, but my adrenalin was pumping. I was excited to have the spirit with me. I asked the spirit questions, but I didn't get any answers.

"You hear stories of spirits like this following people home from investigations. I didn't know if the spirit was really a little girl's spirit or it was another spirit only pretending to be a little girl, and if it should get inside my house, and it was a lying spirit, and was actually an evil spirit, what would it do? So, as a precaution, when I got home I spread a semi-circle of sea salt at the head of the walkway in front of my house, right outside the door of my parked car, which I parked in front of my house at the head of the walkway. Then I sprinkled holy water on the car... I was lucky. As it turned out, nothing came inside my house with me and I never heard the spirit laugh or murmur again. It was gone."

Winged Monsters on the Mount?

Besides ghostly experiences, seeing fleeting figures is not unusual in the woods of Mount Misery at night. One experience recorded on Tribe. net for the world to read tells of a tall, winged being that followed two men in the woods of Mount Misery.

In 2006, two young men ventured to Mount Misery and had an experience they will never forget. Luckily, one of the thrill seekers, who goes by the screen name Shaman Sun, kindly recorded his experience and posted it on the Mothman of Mount Misery thread in the Believe in the Weird Community on Tribe.net.

According to Shaman Sun's post, "Mount Misery Mothman," he and a friend decided to venture into the woods of Mount Misery at night with only "two flashlights, two tape recorders, and our very own five senses." When they were deep into the woods, they heard a strange "ping."

Here's an excerpt from Shaman Sun's amazing story:

"It was then that I saw it.

"Glancing back, I looked to the path. There it was. In the first few seconds that I saw it, it appeared to only be a black shadow, a black cloud of sorts, emerging from the sea of pale light. It stood out clearly from the rest of the forest.

"But then it moved. It appeared to 'stretch' itself out and up, in a moment forming the figure of a tall man. A shadow man, with massive shoulders resembling wings folded back. It had a head, but I saw no eyes. It did not appear to have any legs.

"And it also didn't just watch us leave. It began to head down the trail at an alarming fast rate. At this point, my stomach felt as if it had flipped over. It was chasing us!"

The men reached their car and shot out of the area quickly. In the car they confirmed to each other what they had seen.

According to author Bill Knell, an expert on Mount Misery:

"At least two of the five original Native American Tribes that existed on Long Island considered the area taboo. Notations that I've seen in journals from some of the area's oldest churches indicate that Indians were fearful of the area. They believed that negative forces were at work. Taking the appearance of odd lights on various parts of the Mount as a bad omen, those who did journey through that area sometimes found dead and mutilated animals. A few early settlers experienced much the same thing, finding their cattle or horses dead and strangely mutilated after strange lights were seen in the sky."

By now it should be obvious that something strange is going on in the woods of Mount Misery. It may not be just one paranormal phenomenon allegedly taking place nightly there, but a whole host of varied phenomena, ranging from ghosts to UFOs. What causes these forces to be unleashed in this area of Long Island, in The Long Island Devil's Triangle, is a mystery.

However, the mystery doesn't end here. The forces seem to continue south to the 1,400 acres of greenery of Bethpage State Park, and into Farmingdale and Bethpage, where a creature we dubbed the Long Island Devil has allegedly been seen.

Tortured Mt. Misery Road

A Cauldron of Monsters, Ghouls, Ghosts and Extraterrestrials?

UFO sightings, dark stories of extraterrestrials, appearances by strange humanoids, winged Mothman monsters, ghosts, cries of banshees and long-dead humans, beasts and monsters of the tormented night, Men in Black, and "black ops." military hospitals — all of it has been reported in connection to Mount Misery Road in Melville.

If you follow the stream of stories about Mount Misery Road, you are left to believe it is nothing short of a hellish abyss of ghouls and devils rampaging the night, a place that is exactly how it sounds because of what allegedly goes on there after the sun goes down — pure misery!

Mount Misery Road

A wooden utility pole, with the words "Mt. Misery Rd." stenciled on its side, stands at the corner of Mount Misery and Old Country Roads. This is the spot where some people say Mary was burned at the stake for her sins against the people of Sweet Hollow. This is the only marker for Mount Misery Road. There are no street signs along the mile-long road. The street sign at Old Country Road (first traffic light west of Sweet Hollow Road on Old Country Road) has either been removed in recent years by the town, local residents who are fed up with visitors to the road, or by vandals who stole the sign for a keepsake. What happened in the woods of Mount Misery that makes it such a place of dark legends?

There are those who say the Devil himself visits the woods and flies across the road during the witching hour. Others say a Mothman-like creature with dark bat-like wings takes refuge in the woods of Mount Misery and reveals its burning red eyes in the night to unsuspecting lovers parked at the edge of blackened woods. Yet others claim a madman has been seen crossing the road carrying a bucket full of freshly severed human heads.

Mary, the ghost of nearby Sweet Hollow Road, and the Lady in White, of Sweet Hollow Road, are also said to appear here.

So disturbing are all the legends, stories, and accounts of Mount Misery Road that FearNet.com, a website for horror enthusiasts, named Mount Misery Road one of its top ten Streets of Fear in the United States in 2008. Consider the following excerpt from FearNet's website:

> Locals report seeing the West Virginia legend The Mothman in the area, or at least a similar creature. Various reports indicate that a strange, flying, man-sized creature with moth-like wings and glowing red eyes has been sighted on or above Mount Misery. This same creature has been seen in various places all over the country, but perhaps the famous Mothman was attracted to all the paranormal activity in the area. And though the Mothman is a bizarre phenomenon, not all strange activity from the area has been paranormal.
>
> Local legend asserts that in the early part of the 20th century, travelers passing through the area went missing. Some people reported seeing a disheveled-looking man walking through the woods with a basket full of severed heads! The missing travelers were never found, and the reported man was never captured. Local legend also believes that a military testing facility was built deep in the woods during World War II. Some believe that psychological warfare experiments took place at that testing facility, and cries from patients apparently could be heard during the time.

Strangely, over the ten years that Diane and I have been investigating allegedly haunted Long Island sites, including Mount Misery Road, we have seen very little photographic evidence suggesting the road is as plagued by all the ghosts, ghouls, monsters, and extraterrestrials that so many people claim occupy it at night. In contrast, the woods of Mount Misery and haunted Sweet Hollow Road obviously rage with phenomena — these places abound with evidence of paranormal activity that can actually be captured in photographs.

However, in our experience when there are so many claims and stories about a place such as Mount Misery Road, there is usually some truth behind it. Though the road definitely is dark and lonely in certain places and can scare the hell out of anyone, what most people see when they visit the road during the day is an area of neat housing developments, a day camp for kids, and an enormous tower on the crest of the Mount. Not creatures and ghosts... though there have been unexplained events that have been documented by investigators on Mount Misery Road.

For example, methodical investigators from the well-established Long Island paranormal research group, Long Island Paranormal Investigators (LIPI), recorded a voice at night on Mount Misery Road from their walkie-talkie that was nothing short of the voice one would expect in a horror movie about ghouls coming out of their graves and stomping off in search of fresh human flesh.

Over a walkie-talkie investigators heard a cryptic voice pleading, "Get me out of here!" Then, in another transmission the voice said, "save" as if it was calling to be saved. In yet another walkie-talkie communication the voice said, "I'm burning!"

At one point, a LIPI investigator asked the entity, "What is your name?" The response: "My name is..." and then the voice cut off.

One can only imagine what name the ghoulish voice would have said if the transmission had been completed. These and other EVPs captured at Mount Misery Road can be reviewed on the LIPI website: www.liparanormalinvestigators.com.

The Coney Island Monster

Man or Beast?

One of the strangest stories ever to be told about the shoreline of New York is that of the flying frogman of Coney Island. According to the *New York Times*, many people witnessed a man with wings flying high over Coney Island on a clear, hot day in early September 1880.

"One day last week a marvelous apparition was seen near Coney Island," the September 12, 1880 *New York Times* article began. "At the height of at least a thousand feet in the air the strange object was in the act of flying toward the New Jersey coast. It was apparently a man with bat's wings and improved frog's legs."

The newspaper of record went on to detail what the frogman looked like:

"The face of the man could be distinctly seen, and it wore a cruel and determined expression. The movements made by the object closely resembled those of a frog in the act of swimming with his hind legs and flying with his front legs, Of course, no respectable frog has ever been known to conduct himself in precisely that way; but were a frog to wear a bat's wings, and to attempt to swim and fly at the same time, he would correctly imitate the conduct of the Coney Island monster."

Other Sightings

The *New York Times* reporter went on to compare the sighting of the frogman to similar sightings:

"About a month ago an object of precisely the same nature was seen in the air over St. Louis by a number of citizens who happened to be sober and are believed to be trustworthy. A little later it was seen by various Kentucky persons as it flew across the state. In no instances has it been known to alight, and no one has seen it at a lower elevation than a thousand feet above the surface of the Earth. It is without doubt the most extraordinary and wonderful object that has ever been seen, and there should be no time lost in ascertaining its precise nature, habits, and probable mission.

"That this aerial apparition is a man fitted with practicable wings there is no reason to doubt. Someone has solved the problem of aerial navigation by inventing wings with which a man can sustain himself in the air and direct his flight to any desired point."

These days one has to ask if the flying frogman was actually the infamous Jersey Devil, a being that has plagued the New Jersey Pinelands since 1735. Or could the frogman have been an early sighting of the Long Island Devil, a being that was first reported to us by a man who saw it in 2008 and again in 2009?

The Long Island Devil

LOCATION: Old Quaker Burying Ground (Bethpage, Friends, and Powell cemeteries), Quaker Meeting House Road, Farmingdale.

DIRECTIONS: Take the Long Island Expressway to Exit 48 (Round Swamp Road/Old Bethpage/Farmingdale) and get onto North Service Road. Go .3 miles. Turn left at Round Swamp Road and go 3.5 miles. Bear slight right on Quaker Meeting House Road and go .3 miles. You will see the Quaker Meeting House on your left. Past the meeting house on the left is a cemetery. Directly across from the cemetery is a parking lot on your right for Bethpage State Park Golf Course. Though vehicles can be driven into the cemeteries during the day, for nighttime investigations you might want to park in marked stalls in the parking lot for Bethpage State Park Golf Course. Nobody ever questioned us about parking there and it's easy to get back to your car if you need something. (Additional information: A big problem encountered while investigating cemeteries is that there are no lavatories available. So go before you arrive. Also, bring bug spray in the summer.)

The Guardian of Nellie Backerd's Ghost

A six-foot tall, all-black entity, donning an ominous black cape and Grim Reaper type hood, able to fly up high among the limbs of tall trees, and then disappear at will, has allegedly been spotted at least three times since 2008 near a string of old haunted graveyards in Farmingdale.

The most recent report of this inexplicable and mysterious creature came to us in the windy spring of 2011 by the friend of two witnesses, whom, we were told, refuse to come forward with their incredible story. This friend said the witnesses are a married couple and live in a house in

Bethpage, the hamlet next to Farmingdale. They will not come forward to tell their story because they don't want to be bothered by the public. They also don't want to be labeled as "crazy."

The latter fear is a common problem we have encountered as investigators of the paranormal.

The couple's friend told us her friends saw a black being in their backyard in Bethpage on at least two separate occasions. The creature "ran into the woods," reported this woman, quoting the witnesses.

The description of the alleged monster related to us by this woman, a member of our audience at Farmingdale Public Library where Diane and I were delivering a lecture on March 25, 2011, matched the description by the first witness we interviewed, Patrick Kenney of Farmingdale, who came to us with his fantastic story in 2009.

Psychics involved in a massive investigation to determine the nature of the black being that Kenney saw claim it is the Guardian for the ghost of a girl who is trapped on Earth and will forever haunt the three old graveyards of the Old Quaker Burying Ground unless she can bring her killers to justice. These old cemeteries are strung together in a contiguous line in Farmingdale.

The psychics do not know if the girl whose ghost haunts the cemeteries was buried in one of the Farmingdale graveyards or not. Diane and I have seen instances where ghosts hitchhike, sort of speak, onto other cemeteries where they were not buried, and make themselves known to people.

The night turns black in the graveyards of Old Quaker Burying Ground. When the moon is full, the landscape is bathed in a blue haze.

A local resident, who said he grew up in the area, claimed when he was a kid ghosts ran through the graveyards screaming at night. He said during the 1960s and 1970s he and his friends used to sit up at night inside the graveyards and watch the ghosts and listen to them wail.

Meanwhile, psychics who claim to have spoken to the ghost of the girl who is trapped in the graveyards said she will not leave the hallowed ground until she can bring her killer or killers to justice. The ghost wants the world to know how she was murdered. More importantly, she wants to reveal who her killers are and she wants them punished.

The problem is…her killers are long dead and so is she — and she doesn't even know it.

The Devil's Appearances

Patrick Kenney, a church worker in his late forties from Farmingdale, first reported sightings to us of the strange creature he saw — that we came to dub The Long Island Devil — following a lecture we gave at Farmingdale Public Library in the spring of 2009.

"I didn't know who else to tell," Kenney explained. He stood on the other side of the podium from me at the head of the lecture room after our lecture had concluded and people were saying good-night to each other and talking in small groups about ghosts. "Most people would think I'm nuts!" he added.

To be honest, Diane and I did think Kenney was nuts. I mean, come on, who sees black beings in trees, right? However, we quickly changed our minds about Kenney's sanity when we followed up with a meeting at the exact location in Farmingdale where he claimed to have seen the all-black entity high up in a tree one day while walking his little dog.

"It was crouching on the limb of a tree — high up — watching people having a party in a backyard behind a fence," he told us as we recorded his story on video some months after we gave the lecture in Farmingdale. The leaves on the trees were thick on the day we interviewed him, but when Patrick saw the creature it was spring and the leaves were not yet full.

"I watched it for at least two minutes," he continued. "My dog saw it, too. The creature didn't pay any attention to me or my dog. It just pointed a finger at the people having the party in the backyard. Then it disappeared. It just went *whoosh* and turned into particles or something and was gone!"

The following October, during an interactive segment at another of our biyearly lectures at Farmingdale Public Library, Kenney said in front of the whole audience that he had seen the Devil yet again during another dog walk.

This time the creature was not in a tree, but standing in the middle of a road outside Powell Cemetery, one of the three small graveyards linked together in Farmingdale.

"It was standing in the road, looking down at something," Kenney remembered.

"I watched it for a few seconds," he recalled. "I thought to myself, 'there's that thing again!'"

Before Kenney knew it, the mysterious being he claims appeared in his neighborhood for the second time simply disappeared before his unbelieving eyes.

Patrick Kenney of Farmingdale points to the tree in which he saw the black creature that has been come to be known as The Long Island Devil. Kenney said he saw the entity a second time a year later outside a known haunted cemetery.

The church caretaker carefully marked out the location of the Long Island Devil's second appearance using a fire hydrant as a reference point. He saw that this time the Devil appeared only a stone's throw from the edge of Powell Cemetery.

Powell Cemetery is located at the eastern end of the three graveyards. It's the prettiest of the three cemeteries because of its lush landscape of grass and old trees. Many members of the Powell family are buried in its rich soil. Thomas Powell, a Quaker, settled the area in 1695 after he bought fifteen square-miles of land from local Indian tribes. Places like Bethpage and Farmingdale, and many other hamlets, were areas included in the Bethpage Purchase. Ironically, Thomas Powell is not buried in the family cemetery in Farmingdale, but in a small family graveyard beside a former Grumman plant in Bethpage.

The monster appeared close to the spot where Kenney said his father also once saw the black creature while walking the family dog. But his father, he said, will not speak to us about the Devil.

What resulted from Kenney's two sightings of the Long Island Devil was the largest paranormal investigation ever undertaken on Long Island.

A total of forty investigators were drawn to the irresistible, once-in-a-lifetime alleged Long Island monster case.

Ghost of a Girl Burned at the Stake?

Amazingly, during one of six investigative sessions conducted at the graveyards over the course of three months in the spring of 2010, one experienced psychic-medium claimed to have actually spoken with the spirit of an entity that said it was the ghost of the teenage girl who was murdered.

This happened while the psychic stood in front of many other investigators on a dark night when the wind was near-still. Some of the researchers saw the indistinct white figure of the ghost inside a cluster of trees, while others saw nothing.

According to the medium, the ghost had "long, flowing blond hair and was wearing a blue gown."

To everyone's amazement, the psychic was able to ascertain the ghost's name and other specifics of her life and death as the rest of us watched shadows and movements in the woods.

Psychic-medium Ruth Bahr answers questions about her communication with the ghost of Nellie Backerd during the group's fourth investigative session wrap-up following an extraordinary contact with the ghost of a sixteen year-old girl. Bahr uncovered the tragic story of Nellie's murder and her need to bring her murderers to justice. The ghost told Bahr she was burned at the stake for being a witch.

Shadows in the Woods

The spirit of sixteen-year-old Nellie Backerd told well-known psychic-medium Ruth Bahr from Franklin Square, a member of Long Island Ghost Seekers, that she had been burned at the stake because she was believed to have been a witch.

This killing, the ghost told Bahr, took place in the "nineties," but the ghost did not reveal what century she was referring to before she disappeared.

At one point, as she answered the psychic's questions, Nellie Backerd's apparition grew angry and her visage flared a fiery red. The psychic and some other investigators actually saw the red of the ghost change the color of the area where it stood, and they discussed the event as it was happening.

"She's turning red!" one of the members of the team called out simultaneously.

In all, about twenty people were standing in the area watching the nighttime scene unfold at the edge of the woods behind the Quaker Meeting House in Friends Burial Ground, the middle graveyard in the string. But because Nellie's spirit suddenly faded back into the oblivion of the void from whence she came, the psychic fell just short of extracting information about the exact century the teenager was burned at the stake for being a witch, and by whom.

Investigators were left to speculate whether or not Nellie was burned at the stake for witchcraft in the 1690s, the same decade twenty people were put to death for witchcraft in Salem, Massachusetts, or if it was another century, perhaps the twentieth century?

Officially, there is no record of anybody on Long Island ever being put to death under the old English witchcraft laws, which were severe. Though three Long Islanders were accused of being witches in the 1600s and brought to trial, all three were later acquitted of the witchcraft charges in a New York City court.

Unofficially, anything could have happened in Long Island's woods in the old days.

This same kind of potential for unrecorded violence and killing may be the cause of mysteries that plague not only the graveyards where Nellie Backerd haunts, but the nearby haunted woods of Mount Misery and Sweet Hollow Road, too. After all, there is a legend of Mary from Sweet Hollow who was burned at the stake in the woods of Mount Misery for being an evil witch.

A group of investigators on the third night of the six-night Long Island Devil Investigation look up to the chimney of the Quaker Meeting House in Farmingdale after two psychic mediums — who didn't know each other — said they both psychically saw the same black creature sitting on the edge of the chimney kicking its feet and watching people below. Other investigators saw nothing. The creature disappeared moments later.

In addition, people have seen the ghosts of soldiers and horses on Sweet Hollow Road, as if a battle nobody is aware of ever taking place occurred in the area and left both men and beasts dead, only later to become ghosts.

One fellow told us and our audience at a lecture that he once saw a soldier in what appeared to be Civil War garb cooking food over a small campfire at the edge of Sweet Hollow Road, near the entrance to West Hills Nature Preserve. But when he later returned to the exact spot and took a good look around, there was no sign of the soldier, burned or charred wood, food, or evidence that anyone had ever sat where the soldier sat. Like many other witnesses to strange events on Sweet Hollow Road, the man scratched his head and realized he had seen a ghost.

One of the practices investigators were encouraged to maintain during the Long Island Devil Investigation of 2010 at the Old Quaker Burying Ground in Farmingdale was to submit summaries of their experiences to the group in the days following each of the six investigation sessions. While there were many amazing stories by investigators who participated in the investigation, the summary submitted to the group by psychic-medium Ruth Bahr concerning her experiences with the ghost of Nellie Backerd during the night investigation session of May 16, 2010, is particularly relevant to understanding the inter-dimensional black being that might be the Long Island Devil.

....As we were traveling through the woods I saw something moving on my left side deep in the woods. It moved when I moved, and it stopped when I stopped.

When we got to the Quaker Meeting House I was once again drawn to the back of the house. This time I first saw a shadowy figure by the tree not too far into the woods. It was a hooded figure kind of hovering behind the tree. I was drawn to it and investigator Mark (Koenigsmann) followed close behind me. I told him what I saw and he went deep into the woods. When we got closer to the tree the shadowy figure vanished or went up, I couldn't really see. Investigator Joe (Flammer) came over with his camera and Mark and I both described what we saw. I think it was investigator Barbara (Loiko) who called us back over to the back of the Quaker Meeting House because she heard or saw something in the woods. When we got over to her I thought I heard a woman scream, "No!" from within the woods. Shortly after my attention was drawn upward towards another tree not too far from us in the woods. When I looked up I noticed a shadowy figure sitting in the tree tops. I tried to communicate with it, but no response.

After the third time with no response from the figure in the woods I saw a woman in blue surrounded in a white light. She was 5'7" tall with long flowing blonde hair. I saw the same woman almost a month ago in the same location. I took the opportunity to communicate with her and she did respond to me. She told me she was sixteen years old and that she was burned in a fire. I asked her for a name. She told her name was Nellie. I asked her why she haunted these woods. She said she was bound to the Earth and could not leave until she found the one that burned her. The rest of the investigators asked me if she could reveal herself to them. I told Nellie "Show yourself: We are not here to hurt you!"

Just about everyone in the group saw her when she materialized. Some saw her as a white mist. Others saw her as a white orb or just plain energy. Some of us saw her as a white silhouette. I saw her like I see regular people, but I could not see her face. When asked why she was burned she said the people who burned her thought she was a witch. She said it happened in the "90s," but she did not give a year. Then I heard her say her last name is "Backerd."

Then I asked her about the shadowy figure in the trees. She told me he was her Guardian and she knew him only as The Guardian. She told me he was with her from age six. That he always stayed high up and never came down and he stayed with her through her time of death and continues to stay with her until she is released and she cannot be released until he who burned her is found.

Then the other investigators asked her questions. Through me, I was her voice. I do not remember all the questions that were asked, but after staying with us for some time, she and her Guardian vanished.

This is what I experienced out there tonight. The questions are: Who is the Guardian? Why can he not touch hallowed ground? Why was West Hills Park mentioned? Is the Guardian the Long Island Devil? These are questions we should all ponder....

It should be noted that Bahr's description of the Guardian was confirmed by five other psychics, with a sixth psychic agreeing that a non-human entity dwells in the place that Bahr identified.

Long Island Devil Investigation
Uncovers Paranormal Activity

Several of the enthralled investigators hot on the case of the Long Island Devil were prominent Long Island psychic-mediums who immediately felt spiritual energy in the graveyards and quickly went to work on making contact.

Others among the investigators are some of Long Island's most well-known paranormal researchers.

One member of the team, Peter T. Park from Garden City South, is a cryptozoology specialist with a PhD. from the University of Virginia. Peter conducted extensive research on sightings of creatures similar to the Long Island Devil that have been witnessed by people in different places around the world. He supplied us with information to guide us as the weeks of the investigation continued; and then, at night, he stood with us in the graveyards to search for the alleged monster.

Photo of a paranormal mist stirring beside Quaker Meeting House at the Friend's Burial Ground in Farmingdale. *Photo by North Babylon psychic John Altieri of The Babylon Paranormal Group.*

Yet other investigators who searched the brush, trees, and night sky for the Devil were relatively new to the paranormal investigation scene, but quickly advanced to become experienced veterans on account of the extraordinary amount of spiritual activity that erupted in these cemeteries.

According to at least two of the psychics leading the group with their extraordinary sensitivity, all the investigators who participated in the Long Island Devil Investigation were individually chosen by the spirits and invited to the graveyards to learn of Nellie's gruesome murder and of her need to expose her killers. None of this was an accident, but meant to happen, they said.

Nearly all of the investigators who participated in the investigation saw some forms of apparitions, such as shadow people, darting across the landscape or crouching in a stalking stance in the woods. Others saw mists, ghost lights, or floating orbs.

Additionally, many investigators heard tell-tale signs of spirit activity in the graveyards, such as whispering, murmuring, breathing, whistling, singing, laughing, and crying.

One investigator made note of a grave that he said later disappeared.

Several saw the blank facade of a grave monument suddenly come to life with esoteric words that appeared before their eyes in the cement on the side of a monument, as if a magic show was in progress.

Investigators recorded EVP of disembodied voices and photographed strange images of mists and black figures. David Koenigsann, a thirteen-year-old investigator from Massapequa Park who investigates with his father, conducted an experiment whereby he rolled a blue beach ball onto the top of a grave: we watched the ball vibrate at such a high speed that the slight movements of the ball were barely perceptible. Several of us had to examine the ball repeatedly to make sure we were seeing correctly or if we were misinterpreting the result of a breezes making contact with the ball, thus causing it to vibrate: no, it was not a breeze that was responsible, the ball was vibrating!

Alleged Monster Might Roam a Large Area

Investigators met at night for several hours on each of the six investigation sessions of the Long Island Devil Investigation, conducted over the span of three months in the spring of 2010.

The paranormal researchers combed the three graveyards collectively known as The Old Quaker Burying Ground. The cemeteries are linked together in a contiguous line, making it easy for investigators to move from one cemetery to the other. The names of the cemeteries are Powell, Friends Burial Ground, and Bethpage. All three graveyards are relatively small and bordered on at least one side by woods.

Directly across the street of the cemeteries is Bethpage State Park Golf Course, where we parked our cars. It's the beginning of a 1,400-acre-large area of open space and woods. Only a short distance to the northeast, and linked by strips of greenery, is Suffolk County's West Hills Park, 854-acres of treed land of which West Hills Nature Preserve on Mt. Misery comprises 174 acres.

Is this the reason why winged beings are reportedly seen not only on Mount Misery but also in Farmingdale? Are the wide areas of woods providing a haven for a creature or creatures that have yet to be documented? Or is this entire area a place where spirits take flight by way of a vortex — a sort of Long Island's Devil Triangle?

Are creatures similar to the Jersey Devil or The Mothman living in these vast tracts of Long Island's woods? Or are the winged beings allegedly seen in these areas spiritual entities like Nellie Backerd's Guardian?

Jersey Devil experts claim as many as 2,000 people have in some way either seen or experienced the beast of Leeds, New Jersey since 1735, when it was reportedly born the thirteenth child to a woman who was reputedly impregnated by the Devil himself, as the legend goes.

The Jersey Devil is a monster that supposedly has the head of a horse, a forked tail, the hooves of a goat, and the black wings of a bat. It reportedly terrorized people in the pine barrens of New Jersey for nearly three centuries, and still occasionally is seen in the Pinelands, an area that comprises a third of the state. Reportedly, the monster kills livestock and has been known to swoop down over people in town.

Mothman, on the other hand, is a being that was witnessed in West Virginia. It was reported to stand eight feet tall and have burning red eyes. It's considered a harbinger of doom because it was associated with the Silver Bridge collapse on the Ohio River in December 1967; forty-six people died in that incident.

Is the alleged Long Island Devil masking itself as a tree nodule so it can go undetected? Some of these types of tumors in the nearby woods are enormous. If a winged creature was to mimic one of these tumors, it would be perfectly camouflaged. As long as it doesn't move while it sleeps, no one looking up at it would be the wiser.

Mothman seemed to evaporate following the Silver Bridge tragedy, but for more than a year beforehand, during 1966-1967, it was spotted flying in the area of Point Pleasant, West Virginia. Mothman's appearance coincided with a UFO "flap," or rash, which also abruptly ended when the Silver Bridge crashed into the Ohio River's icy waters. For details, read *The Mothman Prophesies* by John A. Keel. He was the investigator who documented all the events of Point Pleasant, West Virginia, that may ultimately prove so pertinent in our understanding of the alleged entities of Mount Misery and Farmingdale.

Is Entity a Spirit Guide for Murdered Girl's Ghost?

It wasn't until deep into the third month of the Long Island Devil investigation that Ruth Bahr made contact with the spirit of Nellie Backerd again. It was then that she ascertained the nature of the black being that Patrick Kenney may have seen. Bahr was told by the spirit of Nellie Backerd that the black being was a spirit guide protecting Nellie while she is trapped on Earth awaiting justice and revenge against her killers.

How could it be that ghosts are accompanied by spirit guides while stuck on Earth? Nobody can explain this, of course.

Initial research on the name "Nellie Backerd," and variations of spellings of the name, have produced no leads for us to follow-up.

Search for the Long Island Devil Continues

At the time of this writing, the search for the Long Island Devil is ongoing. We are seeking information from residents, workers, and visitors to the Farmingdale-Bethpage area who might have information regarding a winged, black creature allegedly spotted on a road and in trees.

While communications with the spirits of Old Quaker Burying Ground will hopefully reveal more information about Nellie Backerd and her charcoal-black Guardian, it should be remembered that it is truly possible that the ghost of a sad and lonely sixteen-year-old girl is forever wandering the graveyards at night looking to revenge a great wrong done to her.

Watch out for the Guardian.

If you are planning to pursue these spiritual entities on your own, remember that nighttime investigations are extremely hazardous because it's easy to trip and fall on objects in dark graveyards.

Also, crossing the local roads, such as Quaker Meeting House Road, located at the front of the cemeteries, is terribly dangerous. Most people who participated in the Long Island Devil Investigation parked at marked parking stalls belonging to Bethpage State Park Golf Course, located directly across from the graveyards. But be careful if you do this, for we have learned people have been killed on this road by vehicles flying around the bend in front of the graveyards. A lot of people died in car crashes in front of and next to the cemeteries, too, we have been told.

Moreover, we can not assure you that you will be free of police attention. We don't know the cemeteries' official stance on nighttime investigations. But we are confident that if you make a lot of noise and draw attention to yourself in the graveyards at night, you will probably have neighboring homeowners calling the police. If the cops come, you're on your own. Making a lot of noise in a cemetery at night can turn a paranormal investigation into a police investigation.

To contribute information about your own investigations or sightings, please contact The Paranormal Adventurers. In the meantime, stay tuned to updates on this alleged monster case in our future books. Happy Hauntings!

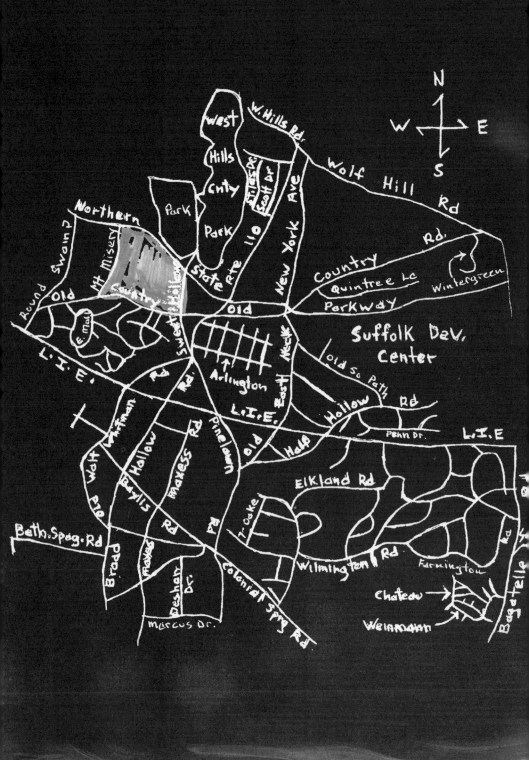

Bibliography

"An Arial Mystery." *New York Times*, September 12, 1880.

Breskin, David. "Kids in the Dark." *Rolling Stone Magazine*, November 22, 1984.

Coleman, Loren and Jerome Clark. *Cryptozoology A to Z*. New York, New York: Simon & Shuster, Inc., 1999.

Flammer, Joseph. "The Fiddler's Tale of Mary of Sweet Hollow Road." Unpublished, © Copyright by Joseph Flammer, 2009.

Flammer, Joseph and Diane Hill. "Frank Greco's Ghost Story of Mary." *The Ghosts of Sweet Hollow Road*, 90-minute DVD. New York, New York: Infinious Publishing, 2009.

Frazer, Sir James. The New Golden Bough. New York, New York: L S.G. Phillips Inc., 1959.

"Ghoul." Encyclopedia Britannica Online, June 27, 2011 (http://www. britannica.com)

"Ghoul." *The New American Roget's College Thesaurus* (prepared by Philip D. Morehead). New York, New York: A Signet Book New American Library, 1985.

"Ghoul," Webster's New Twentieth Century Dictionary, Unabridged, 2nd ed. New York, New York: William Collins Publishing, Inc., 1979.

Guiley, Rosemary Ellen. *The Encyclopedia of Ghosts and Spirits, 2nd ed*. New York, New York: Checkmark Books, 1992.

Haining, Peter. *The Legend and Bizarre Crimes of Spring Heeled Jack*. London, England: Fredrick Muller Ltd., 1977.

Keel, John A. *The Mothman Prophecies*. New York, New York: Tom Doherty Associates, 1975.

Strange Creatures from Time and Space. New York, New York: Fawcett Publications, 1970.

Knell, Bill. "Monsters, Madness, and Mayhem: The Mount Misery Story!" (http://www.homehighlight.org/entertainment-and-recreation/travel-and-leisure/monster-madness-and-mayhem-the-mount-misery-story.html)

Long Island Paranormal Investigators (LIPI): www.liparanormalinvestigators.com

McCloy, James F. and Ray Miller, Jr. *The Jersey Devil*. Moorestown, New Jersey: Middle Atlantic Press, 1987.

McFadden, Robert D. "Youth Found Hanged in L.I. Cell After His Arrest In Ritual Killing." *New York Times*, July 8, 1984.

"Mount Misery Road: Streets of Fear." (http://www.fearnet.com)

"Owlman." *The Unexplained*. (http://leebor2.100webspace.net/winged1.html)

Peterson, Tory. *Peterson First Guide: Birds, a Simplified Field Guide to Common Birds of North America*. New York, New York: Roger, Houghton Mifflin Company, 1980.

Revelation of St. John the Divine 13:18 (King James Version).

Schneck, Robert Damon. *The President's Vampire: Strange Tales of the United States of America*. San Antonio, Texas: Anomalist Books, 2005.

St. Clair, David. *Say You Love Satan*. New York, New York: Dell Publishing, 1987.

"The Beasts Below: Into the Abyss." *Science Illustrated*. Copenhagen, Denmark: Bonnier Publications, September/October 2010.

"The Jersey Devil" (http://theshadowlands.net/jd.htm)

Index